OCR

Biology

Student Workbook

Model Answers: 2012

This model answer book is a companion publication to provide answers for the exercises in the **OCR A2 Biology Student Workbook** 2012 edition. These answers have been produced as a separate publication to keep the cost of the workbook itself to a minimum, as well as to prevent easy access to the answers by students. In most cases, simply the answer is given with no working or calculations described. A few, however, have been provided with more detail because of their difficult nature.

www.biozone.co.uk

ISBN 978-1-877462-85-6

Published by BIOZONE International Ltd

BIOZONE

Additional copies of this Model Answers book may be purchased directly from the publisher

UK & EUROPE:
BIOZONE Learning Media (UK) Ltd.
Bretby Business Park, Ashby Road, Bretby,
Burton upon Trent, DE15 0YZ, **UK**
Telephone: 01283-553-257
Fax: 01283-553-258
Email: sales@biozone.co.uk

AUSTRALIA:
BIOZONE Learning Media Australia
P.O. Box 2841, Burleigh BC,
QLD 4220, **Australia**
Telephone: +61 7-5535-4896
Fax: +61 7-5508-2432
Email: sales@biozone.com.au

REST OF WORLD:
BIOZONE International Ltd.
P.O. Box 13-034,
Hamilton 3251, **New Zealand**
Telephone: +64 7-856-8104
Fax: +64 7-856-9243
Email: sales@biozone.co.nz

Contents

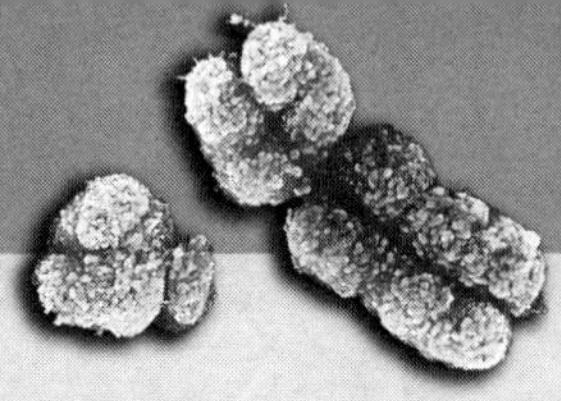

Contents

Contents

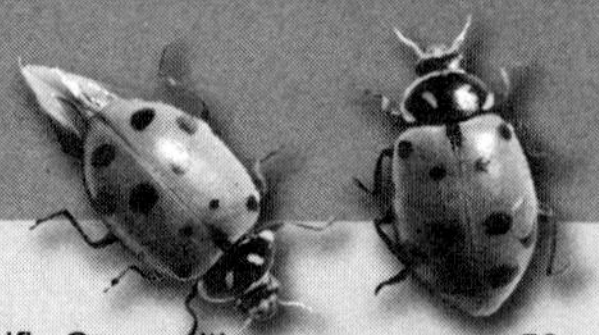

Designing Your Experiment (page 9)

1. (a) Growing just one plant per pot removes the confounding effects of competition between plants (this would occur if plants were grown together).
   (b) The physical layout minimises any effects due to position of the pots on the bench. No one treatment is always near the edge or in the centre. **Teacher's note**: Physical layout can affect the outcome of experimental treatments, especially those involving growth responses in plants. Physical conditions may vary considerably with different placements along a lab bench (near the window vs central), so treatments should be arranged so that all treatments, on average, are similarly affected.
2. The best way to account for natural variability between individuals is to increase the number of individuals you use in each treatment (sample size, *n*).
3. (a) Replication accounts for unforeseen effects in your set-up, i.e. allows you to evaluate the effects of **nuisance** variables over which you have no control.
   (b) Replication is limited by the amount of equipment, space, and/or time you have available.
   (c) You can compensate for a lack of replication by repeating the entire experiment several more times. This may be practicable only if the investigation does not involve lengthy growth responses. Checklist to be completed by the student.

Designing Your Field Study (page 11)

1. (a) An appropriate size of the sampling unit enables you to effectively sample the organisms involved. Collect enough data for the samples to be representative of the population(s) involved, without extra, unnecessary data collection.
   (b) Recognising assumptions is critical to asking appropriate questions in a study. For even the simplest of studies, some background information is important. Making some reasonable assumptions allows you to focus on the questions that you really want to answer and offer plausible explanations if your results do not support your predictions.
   (c) Apart from standard moral obligations to do no damage, consideration of the environment is essential to being able to justify any repeat of your work, and to ensure that any repeat takes place in the same system.
   (d) Organisms should always be returned to the same area to avoid introducing new organisms into regions where they may previously have been absent, and to minimise the impact of sampling on the area being investigated.
   (e) As with size of sampling unit, the total area sampled should be appropriate to the size of the organism(s) being sampled and the questions being asked. **Example**: In a study of altitudinal zonation, it is clearly inappropriate to take a very short transect in a small area, as this would not be representative of community changes.
2. To test quadrat size it would be necessary to sample using a series of quadrats of increasing size. The cumulative number of species recorded after each successive increase in quadrat size could be plotted on a simple graph. The optimum quadrat size occurs when the number of species recorded stops increasing. **Teacher's note:** A smaller size may be acceptable if you are prepared to only record dominant species. However, this carries a risk that trends between different areas may be missed.

   Checklist to be completed by the student.

Qualitative Practical Work: Biological Drawings (page 13)

Task: Student's own drawing. Points to note:

- Cells should be drawn with unbroken lines and not overlapping.
- Cell borders may sometimes be inferred from the positions of the nuclei.
- Structures to label include tubule lumen, cuboidal cells lining tubules, Bowman's capsule, squamous epithelium lining capsule, lumen of capsule.

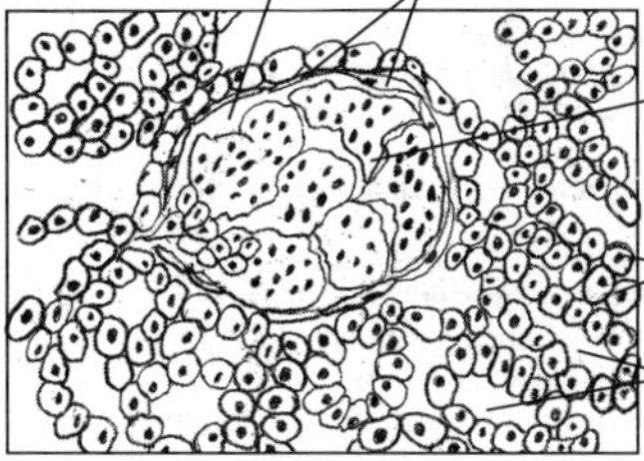

Qualitative Practical Work: Seaweed Zonation (page 14)

1. (a) Percentage cover of each seaweed species.
   (b) Seaweed vigour and degree of dessication.
2. Column graph as below:

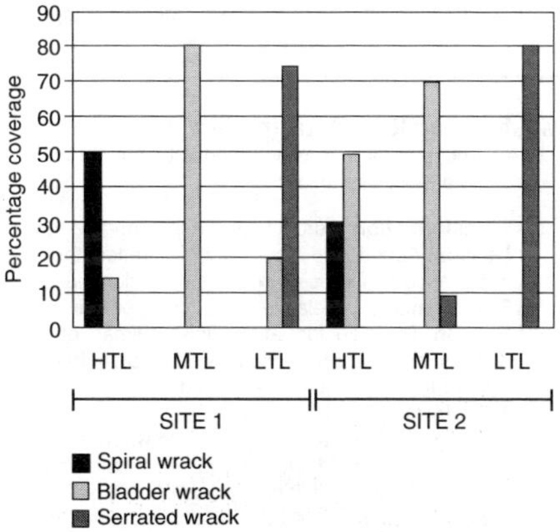

3. Spiral wrack is the most tolerant of long exposure periods, where it grows vigorously despite showing some evidence of desiccation. Bladder wrack grows vigorously throughout the midlittoral and is relatively tolerant of exposure, only showing signs of desiccation higher on the shore where exposure times are longer.

Serrated wrack is intolerant of exposure and grows vigorously at the LTL but shows signs of desiccation above this and cannot compete with the more tolerant bladder wrack.

4. Quadrat position was staggered for the two sites to give a better indication of the extent of each species' distribution. The disadvantage is that the sites cannot be directly compared.

A Quantitative Practical Task (page 15)

1. Aim: To investigate the effect of substrate on the rate of yeast fermentation.
2. Possible hypotheses:
   Some carbohydrates will be more suitable substrates for yeast fermentation than others.
   Rate of yeast fermentation will be greater when grown on glucose than on any other carbohydrate.
3. (a) Independent variable: Time.
   (b) Values: 0-30 minutes in 5 minute intervals.
   (c) Unit: minute
4. (a) Dependent variable: Volume of CO_2 produced.
   (b) Unit: cm^3
5. (a) Each substrate represents a treatment.
   (b) Sample size for each treatment = 1
   (c) Experimental design could be improved by increasing the sample size at each treatment (i.e having two or more set ups for each treatment). Ideally, these would be run at the same time, but usually constraints on equipment preclude this.
6. It would have been desirable to have had an extra set up with no substrate because this would act as the control to demonstrate the amount of fermentation occurring in the absence of substrate (assumed none).
7. (a) pH was maintained by buffers at 4.5. Monitor using a pH meter (indicator paper is not accurate enough).
   (b) Temperature maintained at 24°C. Monitor using a thermometer or temperature logger.

Transforming Raw Data (page 17)

1. The purpose of data transformation is to convert raw data into a more useful form.
2. (a) **Transformation**: Percentage (i.e. percentage cover)
   Reason: Abundance alone might not reflect the importance of a species in terms of its dominance.
   (b) **Transformation**: Relative value (cm^3 per unit mass)
   Reason: This transformation allows animals of different body size to be compared meaningfully without the influence of their actual body size.
   (c) **Transformation**: Reciprocal
   Reason: Provides a measure of rate where the data have been recorded over very different time periods (time taken for precipitation to occur). It is difficult to compare values where the time scale is different for each recording.
   (d) **Transformation**: Rate
   Reason: Data may have been recorded over different time periods. A rate allows the production of CO_2 to be compared per unit of time over all temperatures.
3. Performing data transformations:
   (a) Incidence of cyanogenic clover in different regions:

Clover type	Frost free No.	Frost free %	Frost prone No.	Frost prone %	Totals
Cyanogenic	124	78	26	18	150
Acyanogenic	35	22	115	82	150
Total	159	100	141	100	300

   (b) Plant transpiration loss:

Time / min	Pipette arm reading / cm^3	Plant water loss / cm^3 min^{-1}
0	9.0	-
5	8.0	0.20
10	7.2	0.16
15	6.2	0.20
20	4.9	0.26

   (c) Photosynthetic rate at different light intensities:

Light intensity / %	Average time / min	Reciprocal of time / min^{-1}
100	15	0.067
50	25	0.040
25	50	0.020
11	93	0.011
6	187	0.005

   (d) Frequency of size classes of eels:

Size class / mm	Frequency	Relative frequency / %
0-50	7	2.6
50-99	23	8.5
100-149	59	21.9
150-199	98	36.3
200-249	50	18.5
250-299	30	11.1
300-349	3	1.1
Total	270	100.0

Data Presentation (page 19)

1. The difference between the two means (labelled A) is not significant. The two means are not significantly different because the 95% CIs overlap. The mean at 4 gm^{-3} has such a large 95% CI we cannot be confident that it is significantly different from the mean at 3 gm^{-3} with the very small 95% CI.
2. Graphs and tables provide different ways of presenting information and each performs a different role. Tables summarise raw data. Graphs present information in a way that makes any trends or relationships in the data apparent. Tables provide an **accurate** record of the data values (raw or calculated), which may not be easily obtained from a graph. They can also show any data transformations, descriptive statistics, and results of statistical tests. Both are useful for different reasons.

Types of Graphs (page 20)

1. (a) A point well outside the main spread of the data.
   (b) Outliers can arise where there has been undetected experimental error (e.g. wrong reading). They can indicate sample contamination (e.g. a different species). Occasionally, they can represent real phenomena worth further study.
   (c) Where experimental error is suspected, outliers can legitimately be excluded. In other cases, it is valid to exclude extreme outliers that will bias the statistical result from an otherwise "tight" data set.

2. (a) **Line graph**. Reason: Data are continuous, and one variable is dependent on the other.
   (b) **Bar graph**. Reason: One variable is categorical (discontinuous), the other is continuous.
   (c) **Histogram**. Reason: Data are continuous. One variable is arranged in class intervals, the other is a frequency (count).

3. The class interval should reflect the degree of precision to which the data have been recorded (e.g. if weights are measured to 0.1 kg, the class interval should reflect this). An inappropriate interval may not include all data or it may be unnecessarily precise.

Interpreting Sample Variability (page 22)

1. (a) 496/689 values within ± 1sd of the mean = 72% (48±7.8, i.e. between 40.2 and 55.8)
   (b) 671//689 values within ± 2 sd of the mean = 97% (48± 15.6, i.e. between 32.4 and 63.6)
   (c) The data are very close to being normally distributed about the mean (normal distribution + 67% of values lie within 1sd of the mean and 95% of values lie between 2 sd of the mean).

2. The mean and the median are very close.

3. N = 30 data set
   (a) **Mean** = 49.23
   (b) **Median** = 49.5
   (c) **Mode** = 38
   (d) **Sample variance** =129.22
   (e) **Standard deviation** = 11.37

4. N = 50 data set
   (a) **Mean** = 61.44
   (b) **Median** = 63
   (c) **Mode** = 64
   (d) **Sample variance** = 14.59
   (e) **Standard deviation** = 3.82

5. Frequency histogram for the N=50 perch data set.

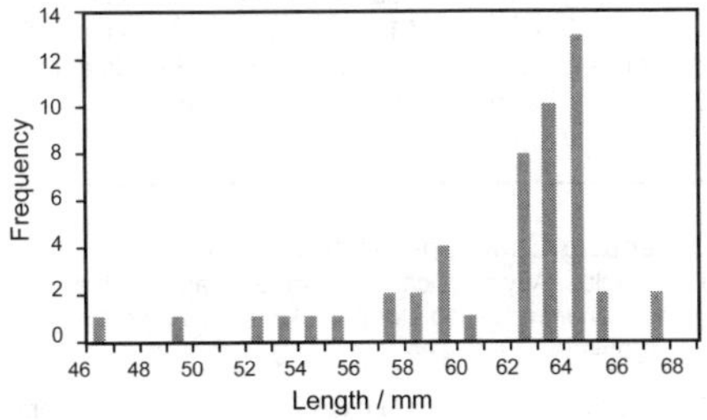

Frequency histogram for the N = 30 perch data set.

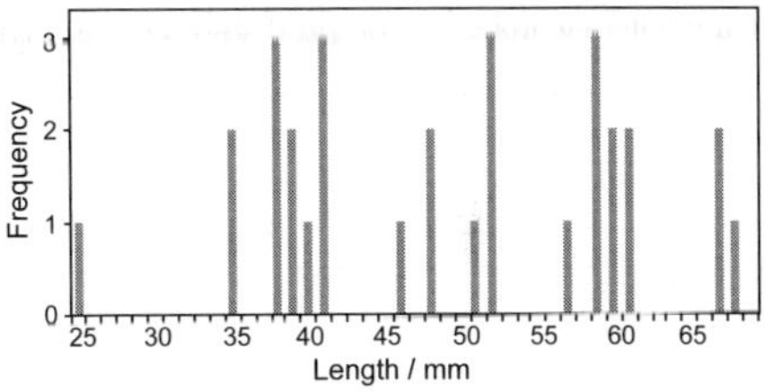

6. (a) The mean and median are very close to each other for the N=30 data set. There is a larger difference between the mean and median values obtained in the N=50 data set.
   (b) The standard deviation obtained for the N=30 set is much larger (11.37) compared to only 3.82 for the larger N=50 data set.
   (c) The N=30 data set more closely resembles the complete data set. The mean and median are quite close to those of the original data set. The mean, median and mode for the N=50 data set are considerably higher than those statistics for the complete data set. The sample variance and standard deviation values for the complete data set fall between those of the two smaller data sets.

7. (a) The frequency histogram for the N=30 data set shows a relatively normal distribution of data. M- The frequency histogram for the N=50 data set shows a non-normal distribution which is skewed to the right (negative skew).
   (b) The person who collected the sample in the N=30 data set used equipment and techniques designed to collect fish randomly. As a result, a normal distribution of fish sizes was obtained by their sampling methods. M- Fish collection for the N=50 sample set was biased. The mesh size used did not retain smaller fish, so a larger proportion of bigger fish were collected. When plotted, the data presented as a negative skew.

Evaluating Your Results (page 24)

1. $C_6H_{12}O_6 \rightarrow C_2H_5OH + 2CO_2$

2. Calculated rate of CO_2 production, group 1:
   (a) None: 0 cm^3min^{-1} or 0 cm^3s^{-1}
   (b) Glucose: 0.443 cm^3min^{-1} or 7.4×10^{-3} cm^3s^{-1}
   (c) Maltose: 0.24 cm^3min^{-1} or 4.0×10^{-3} cm^3s^{-1}
   (d) Sucrose: 0.191 cm^3min^{-1} or 3.2×10^{-3} cm^3s^{-1}
   (e) Lactose: 0.029 cm^3min^{-1} or 4.8×10^{-4} cm^3s^{-1}

3. Calculated rate of CO_2 production, group 2:
   (a) None: 0 cm^3min^{-1} or 0 cm^3s^{-1}
   (b) Glucose: 0.271 cm^3min^{-1} or 4.5×10^{-3} cm^3s^{-1}
   (c) Maltose: 0.211 cm^3min^{-1} or 3.5×10^{-3} cm^3s^{-1}
   (d) Sucrose: 0.194 cm^3min^{-1} or 3.2×10^{-3} cm^3s^{-1}
   (e) Lactose: 0 cm^3min^{-1} or 0 cm^3s^{-1}

4. The assumptions made are that 24°C and pH 4.5 provide suitable (even optimal) conditions for yeast fermentation. This is reasonable as it has been stated in the background that the literature cites warm, slightly acidic conditions as optimal for baker's yeast.

Cumulative volume of CO_2 produced over 90 minutes by yeast grown on different carbohydrate sources.

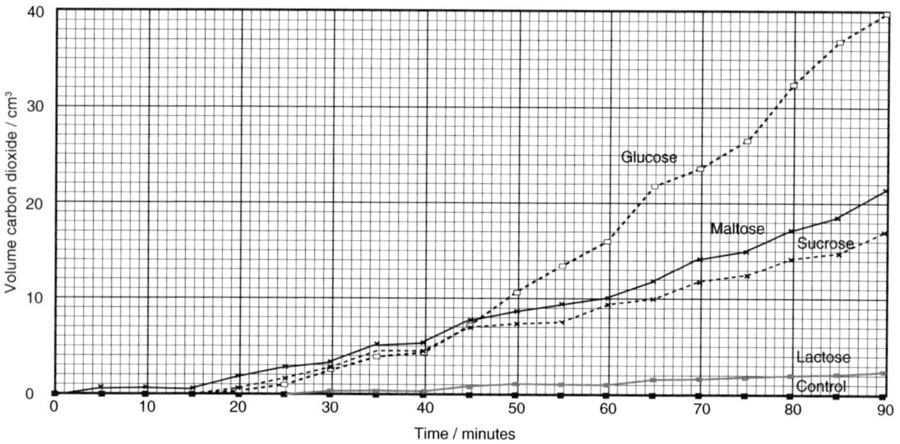

5. Graph of Group 1's results: see above.

6. (a) The fermentation rates were greatest for the substrate glucose, with a CO2 yield approximately twice that for maltose and sucrose. Maltose and sucrose were similar to each other, while the rate of fermentation on lactose was minimal.
   (b) Glucose is the preferred substrate (directly available as a fuel). Maltose (glucose-glucose) and sucrose (glucose-fructose) must first be hydrolysed before the glucose is available (the fructose from sucrose must also be isomerised to glucose). This accounts for the lower fermentation rates on these substrates. Lactose is a poor fuel, presumably because yeast lack the enzyme to hydrolyse the galactose and glucose that form this disaccharide.

7. (a) Column chart comparing results of the two groups.

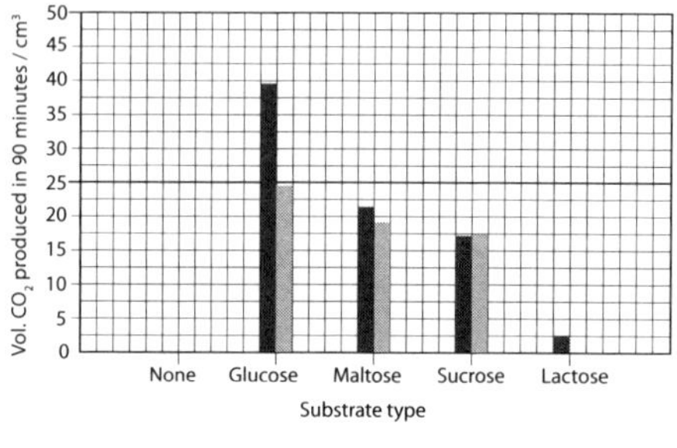

   (b) Main points to note are that both groups had results of similar magnitude for maltose and sucrose. Group 1's fermentation rates were much higher on glucose but group 2's were only a little higher on glucose than those for maltose and sucrose. Group 1 had some fermentation response for lactose, but group 2 had the same result as for no substrate.
   (c) Both groups had very active fermentation on glucose, sucrose, and maltose. Group 1's finding that yeast fermented lactose is probably erroneous as yeast lack the enzyme required to hydrolyse lactose to component monosaccharides. The fact that group 2 did not obtain any CO_2 production for lactose suggests that group 1's lactose was contaminated with some other substrate, accounting for a low level of activity. Group 1's very high rates of activity on glucose could be attributable to using a different batch of (fresher) yeast, but this would have to be tested further.

8. The main improvement to the experiment would be to repeat the experiment 3 or 4 times under the same conditions, or run replicates, so that a mean volume and rate of CO_2 production could be calculated for each substrate. This would help to account for some of the variability. Ensuring that all tests are made with the same batch of yeast and that the yeast is still active (i.e. not old stock) would also be worthwhile. Students should also note a procedure to ensure no cross contamination between substrates.

KEY TERMS: Mix and Match (page 26)

Accuracy (O), Biological drawing (X), Control (C), Controlled variables (A), Data (D), Dependent variable (I), Graph (R), Histogram (L), Hypothesis (M), Independent variable (B), Mean (H), Measurement (P), Median (N), Mode (E), Observation (S), Parameter (G), Precision (Z), Qualitative data (U), Quantitative data (J), Raw data (Q), Sample (V), Scientific method (T), Standard deviation (K), Trend (of data) (F), Variable (Y)

Detecting Changing States (page 29)

1. Stimulus: Any physical or chemical change in the environment, capable of provoking a response in an organism.

2. (a) and (b) any from the examples provided (or others). Answers provided as stimulus (receptor):
   (a) External stimuli and their receptors: Light (photoreceptor cells); gravity (hair cells/vestibule

of the inner ear); sound/vibration (hair cells in the cochlea of the inner ear); airborne chemicals (olfactory receptors in the nose); dissolved chemicals (taste buds); external pressure (dermal pressure receptors, e.g. Pacinian corpuscle, Meissner's corpuscles); pain (nerve endings in the dermis); temperature (nerve endings in the skin).

(b) Internal stimuli and their receptors: Blood pH/ carbon dioxide level (chemoreceptors in blood vessels); blood pressure (baroreceptors); stretch (proprioreceptors, e.g. muscle spindle).

Cell Signalling (page 30)

1. (a) **Endocrine signalling**, where a hormone is carried in the blood between the endocrine gland/organ where it is produced to target cells.
   (b) **Paracrine signalling**, where cell signalling molecules are released to act on target cells in the immediate vicinity, e.g. at synapses or between cells during development.
   (c) **Autocrine signalling**, where cells produce and react to their own signals (e.g. growth factors from T cells stimulate the production of more T cells).

2. The three signalling types all have in common some kind of chemical messenger or signal molecule (ligand) and a receptor molecule (on the target cells, which may or may not be on the cell producing the signal).

Principles of Homeostasis (page 31)

1. **Receptors** (detect stimuli), **control and coordination centre** (integration of signals and coordination of response), **effectors** (implement appropriate response).

2. Negative feedback mechanisms enable maintenance of a steady state internal environment despite fluctuations in the external environment (e.g. rising air temperature). Negative feedback mechanisms are self-correcting so that physiological systems are stabilised against excessive change.

3. (a) Positive feedback has a role in accelerating a physiological process to bring about a particular required response. Examples include (1) elevation in body temperature (fever) to accelerate protective immune responses, (2) positive feedback between oestrogen and LH to leading to an LH surge and ovulation, (3) positive feedback between oxytocin and uterine contractions: oxytocin causes uterine contraction and stretching of the cervix, which causes more release of oxytocin and so on until the delivery of the infant.
   (b) Positive feedback is inherently unstable because it causes an escalation in the physiological response, pushing it outside the tolerable physiological range. Compare this with negative feedback, which is self correcting and causes the system to return to the steady state.
   (c) Positive feedback loops are normally ended by a resolution of situation causing the initial stimulation. For example, the positive feedback loop between oestrogen and LH leading to ovulation is initiated by high oestrogen levels and ended when these fall quickly after ovulation, prompting a resumption of negative feedback mechanisms. In childbirth, once the infant is delivered, the stretching of the cervix ceases and so too does the stimulation for more oxytocin release.
   (d) When positive feedback continues unchecked, it can lead to physiological collapse. One example includes unresolved fever. If an infection is not brought under control (e.g. by the body's immune system mechanisms or medical intervention), body temperature will continue to rise and can lead to seizures, neurological damage, and death.

4. Sometimes the metabolic responses required to maintain a steady state are too disparate to be brought about by one hormone; it is more physiologically efficient to control responses in different directions with **counter-regulatory hormones**. This is especially true when the homeostatic process is naturally subject to sudden wide variations, which require different responses to stabilise. For example, insulin is released in response to elevated blood sugar and induces cellular uptake of glucose and synthesis of glycogen. Glucagon is released in response to low blood glucose and induces release of glucose from stores.

Maintaining Homeostasis (page 33)

1. Two mechanisms operating to restore homeostasis after infection ((a) and (b) any two of):
   - Immune system response with the production of antibodies against the antigens of the pathogen (humoral response).
   - Immune system response with the production of T cells which recognise the antigens of the pathogen and destroy them directly (cell-mediated response).
   - Local inflammatory response (redness, pain, swelling, heat) at the site of infection.
   - Fever (widespread increase in body temperature).
   - The production of antimicrobial substances like interferon and interleukin-1.
   - Phagocytosis of pathogen by white blood cells.

   All the above aim to destroy the pathogen and/or its toxins and assist a return to homeostasis.

For Q. 2.-4., more explanatory detail than required is given.

2. Mechanisms by which responses to stimuli are brought about and coordinated:
   (a) **Hormonal response** to stimuli: Endocrine glands respond to a stimulus (e.g. a nerve impulse or another hormone or metabolite) by producing hormones which bring about an appropriate physiological response. **For example**, nervous stimulation of the adrenal glands when the body receives a stressful stimulus causes the release of adrenaline. This hormone causes mobilisation of glucose in muscle and liver cells, increases heart rate and directs blood away from nonessential organs. These responses help the body react to the stress situation.
   (b) **Nervous response** to stimuli: Direct stimulation of nerves from a sensory receptor causes a reaction to the stimulus. This may be a response requiring interpretation of the message by the brain or it may be a reflex (an automatic response to a stimulus involving only 2 or 3 neurones), e.g. pain withdrawal.

3. Maintaining water and ion balance by:
   (a) Water and ions are taken in with food and drink, helping to replace that lost through urine, faeces, and sweat. The digestive organs and all of the digestive hormones (e.g. amylase in the mouth,

pepsin in the stomach, trypsin in the small intestine) are all involved in breaking down food and facilitating absorption into the bloodstream.

(b) The kidney is the primary regulator of fluid and ions. When large quantities of fluid must be excreted, the kidney produces large amounts of dilute urine. When water must be conserved, small amounts of concentrated urine are produced. ADH (antidiuretic hormone) causes more water to be reabsorbed from the kidney (causing a more concentrated urine). ADH increases when blood water levels are low. Essential ions (and glucose) are retained by active reabsorption from the kidney tubules. Another hormone, aldosterone from the adrenal glands, increases the absorption of sodium ions.
Note: Water and ions are lost via sweat and water is lost in breathing. These losses are compensated for by the homeostatic role of the kidney. Note that sweating is a mechanism for thermoregulation. It is not usually an important way to rid the body of excessive water and salts.

4. Regulating respiratory gases during exercise by:
   (a) **Increasing breathing rate**. This increases both the rate of oxygen entering the lungs and the rate at which carbon dioxide leaves. It also increases the rate of loading and unloading of oxygen and carbon dioxide into and out of the bloodstream.
   (b) **Increasing the heart rate**. This increases blood flow which facilitates the loading and unloading of oxygen and carbon dioxide into and out of the bloodstream. It also increases the speed of delivery of oxygen to working tissues (e.g. muscles) and speeds up the removal of carbon dioxide and other waste products of metabolism.

Nervous Regulatory Systems (page 35)

1. (a) The **sensory receptors** receive sensory information (information about the environment) and respond by generating an electrical response (message).
   (b) The **central nervous system** (CNS) processes the sensory input and coordinates an appropriate response (through motor output).
   (c) A system of **effectors** bring about an appropriate response.
   Note: Together these systems function to bring about appropriate (adaptive) responses to the environment so that homeostasis (steady state) is maintained.

2. (a) and (b) any two in any order:
   - Nervous control involves transmission across synapses, hormonal control involves transport of chemicals in the blood.
   - Nervous control is rapid, hormonal control is slower.
   - Nervous control acts in the short term and its effects are short lived, hormonal control is longer acting.
   - Nervous control is direct and through specific pathways, hormonal control is widespread, affecting target cells throughout the body (although these may be quite specific).
   - Nervous control causes muscular action directly, hormonal control generally acts by changing metabolic activity.

Hormonal Regulatory Systems (page 36)

1. (a) **Antagonistic hormones**: Two hormones that have contrasting (counteracting) effects on metabolism. Examples: insulin and glucagon, parathormone (increases blood calcium) and calcitonin (lowers blood calcium).
   (b) In general principle, the product of a series of (hormone controlled) reactions controls its own production by turning off the pathway when it reaches a certain level. If there is too little of the product, its production is switched on again.

2. Only the target cells have the appropriate receptors on the membrane to respond to the hormone. Other (nontarget) cells will not be affected.

3. (a) Hormones must circulate in the blood to reach the target cells and a metabolic response must be initiated. This takes some time.
   (b) Hormones bring about a metabolic change and often start a sequence of cascading, interrelated events. Once started, these events take time to conclude. Nervous responses continue only for the time that the stimulation continues.

Control of Body Temperature (page 37)

1. (a) A **homeothermic endotherm** maintains a constant (usually high) body temperature despite environmental fluctuations. It does this using internal sources of energy (metabolic activity).
   (b) Many terrestrial lizards and snakes regulate their body temperature to within quite narrow limits using behavioural mechanisms. Their body temperature does not simply fluctuate with ambient temperature.

2. (a) Letting body temperature fluctuate with the environment saves a great deal of energy because the animal does not have to maintain body temperature against environmental variation.
   (b) Ectothermy represents an energy saving since ectotherms are not physiologically committed to maintaining a high metabolic rate. Lower metabolic rates are advantageous when food supplies are low (less energy is required to sustain the animal).

3. Endotherms that undergo torpor usually do so when food supplies are scarce and/or when the metabolic cost of maintaining activity is likely to be prohibitively high (e.g. during very cold weather). Lowering metabolic rates at these times saves energy and allows them to survive until conditions are more favourable.

4. (a) Ectotherm's body temperature increases steadily with increasing ambient temperature. Endotherms maintain a high, constant body temperature despite changes in the environmental temperature.
   (b) An poikilothermic ectotherm would be restricted to temperatures below about 40-45°C because above this point its body temperature would continue to rise to a state of physiological heat stress.
   (c) Optimum temperature range for an endotherm is from 18° or 19°C to 36°C. Between these temperatures, oxygen consumption, and therefore energy expenditure, is lowest.
   (d) At temperatures below 15°C the energetic costs of thermoregulation for an endotherm increase markedly because the environmental temperature is low compared with the preferred constant

body temperature and more energy is required to maintain body temperature against heat loss. At temperatures above 35°C the energetic costs of thermoregulation also increase because large amounts of energy begin to be used to dissipate excess heat and prevent further heat gain.
(e) For ectotherms, the energetic costs of temperature regulation increase steadily with the environmental temperature because as the environmental temperature increases so too does the metabolic rate of the animal. Increased metabolic rate equates to increased energetic expenditure and higher oxygen consumption.

Mechanisms of Thermoregulation (page 39)

1. (a) Water transmits heat away from the body very rapidly, therefore it has a great cooling capacity.
(b) Any two of: Countercurrent heat exchange systems in fins and flippers, insulated body surfaces of thick fat, large body size.
(c) Large body size reduces the surface area (compared to volume) over which heat can be lost.
(d) Any of: High heat production through high metabolic rate, consumption of large amounts of food, hibernation or torpor during winter periods.

2. (a) Thick hair reduces heat loss by trapping an insulating layer of air between the animal and the cooler environment. The insulating layer of hair also reduces heat gain from the environment.
(b) Different fur thicknesses allow an animal to expose or cover thinner areas to allow for greater of lower heat loss depending on needs.
(c) Related species at low altitude could be expected to have less thick and less dense fur covering than animals at high altitude.
(d) They have a thick layer of fat (blubber) underneath the skin. In addition, they are usually large.

3. (a) Use of countercurrent heat exchanges in fast swimming fish allows them to maintain a higher operating temperature in their main swimming muscles. This enables faster metabolic activity and fast, sustained swimming.
(b) These animals ingest large volumes of flesh in their diet, without chewing. A higher temperature around the gut allows them to increase the rate of digestion so that assimilation rates do not lag too much behind the rate at which food is ingested.

4. (a) Animals may group together to retain body heat. By creating a large single mass, heat loss is reduced.
(b) Penguins, honeybees, livestock (sheep, cattle).

Thermoregulation in Humans (page 41)

1. Body temperature reduced by (a and b any two of): • Sweating (cooling by evaporation) • Reducing activity • Behavioural mechanisms such as removing clothing or seeking shade • Increasing blood flow to skin (leads to increased radiation from the skin surface) .

2. (a) **Hypothalamus**: Monitors temperature changes in the body and coordinates appropriate responses to counteract the changes.
(b) **Skin**: Detects changes in skin temperature and relays the information to the hypothalamus. In response to input from the hypothalamus, muscles and capillaries in the skin act as effectors to bring about an appropriate thermoregulatory response.
(c) **Nervous input to effectors**: (from hypothalamus) brings about (through stimulation of muscles) an appropriate thermoregulatory response (e.g. raising hairs, constricting blood vessels).
(d) **Hormones**: Mediate a change in metabolic rate through their general action on body cells (adrenaline and thyroxine increase metabolic rate).

Hypothermia (page 42)

1. Exposure to low temperatures even for a short time without insulation will lead to hypothermia. Even temperatures of 15 to 20°C may cause hypothermia if a person is exposed long enough without protection. Exposure to water will cause hypothermia far more quickly than the same temperature in air as heat is more easily conducted away from the body.

2 (a) Short and stocky
(b) A short, stocky shape has a lower SA:V ratio and so loses heat more slowly.

3. Methods include passive rewarming (using a person's own body heat) for mild hypothermia, active external rewarming (using external heating such as a hot water bottle) for moderate hypothermia and active internal rewarming (using devices to warm body fluids internally) for severe hypothermia. Using an incorrect method may cause the body dilate blood vessels too quickly and so cause a reduction in blood pressure as well as a further drop in body temperature.

The Basis of Sensory Perception (page 46)

1. Sensory receptors convert stimulus energy (e.g. electromagnetic radiation) into electrochemical energy (a change in membrane potential).

2. Sensory receptors all rely on altering the flow of ions across the plasma membrane and producing localised changes in membrane potential (receptor potentials).

3. When the sensory receptor cell is stimulated, specific ion channels in its plasma membrane open or close, altering the membrane potential and causing a localised receptor potential (this may be a depolarisation or hyperpolarisation). The receptor potential spreads to a region of the cell where an action potential is generated (or neurotransmitter is released and an action potential is then generated in a post synaptic cell).

4. (a) Receptor potentials are localised changes in membrane potential and are graded (of different sub-threshold magnitude). Unlike action potentials they are not self-propagating.
(b) Receptor potentials can sum together because they are graded. When graded responses are generated close together in time, they will sum to reach the threshold more readily and so generate action potentials more frequently.

Neurone Structure and Function (page 47)

1. Missing answers as follows:
   Length of fibres:
   Sensory neurone: Axon has two branches, one (usually) shorter central branch and one longer peripheral branch.
   Motor neurone: Many short branching dendrites, a (usually) long axon.
   Function:
   Sensory neurone: Carries impulses fro a sensory receptor to the CNS.
   Motor neurone: Carries impulses from the CNS to effectors (muscles or glands).

2. (a) Myelination increases the speed of impulse conduction.
   (b) Oligodendrocytes
   (c) Schwann cells
   (d) Neurones in the PNS frequently have to transmit over long distances so speed of impulse conduction is critical to efficient function.

3. Myelin prevents ions from entering or leaving the axon along myelinated segments and so prevents leakage of charge across the neurone membrane. The current is carried in the cytoplasm so that the action potential at one node (gap in the sheath) is sufficient to trigger an action potential at the next. Myelin has another advantage too in reducing energy expenditure since fewer ions overall need to be pumped to restore resting potential after an action potential has passed.

4. (a) Faster conduction speeds enable more rapid responses to stimuli.
   (b) Increasing axon diameter increases conduction velocity because it reduces the longitudinal resistance, so local currents can spread further.

5. The destruction of the myelin prevents those (previously myelinated) axons from conducting. Without insulation, the neurone membrane leaks ions and the local current is attenuated and insufficient to depolarise the next node. Note: myelinated axons only have gated channels at their nodes, so action potentials can only be generated at node regions in those axons that were previously myelinated.

Action Potentials (page 49)

1. An action potential is a self-regenerating depolarisation (electrochemical signal) that allows excitable cells (such as muscle and nerve cells) to carry a signal over a (varying) distance.

2. (a) The ability to conduct electrical impulses.
   (b) They cannot conduct electrical impulses.

3. (a) Depolarisation: Na^+ channels open and Na^+ ions flood into the cell.
   (b) Repolarisation: Na^+ channels close, K^+ channels open and K^+ ions move out of the cell.

4. An **action potential** passes along a nerve because the depolarisation occurring in one region of the axon makes the next region of the axon more permeable to sodium ions (and more likely to conduct the impulse).

5. Because the refractory period makes the neurone unable to respond for a brief period after an action potential has passed, the impulse can pass in only one direction along the nerve (away from the cell body).

6. NOTE: Attentive students will notice that this trace does not perfectly match the idealised schematic of an action potential (namely the hyperpolarisation does not fall below threshold and resting potential is more positive than the starting resting potential). Differences in electrophysiological techniques used in recording lead to departures from the schematic. In this case, the real action potential is sitting atop a voltage offset caused by the current pulse used to stimulate the axon.

   (a) B: Membrane depolarisation
   D: Hyperpolarisation
   E: Return to resting potential
   C: Repolarisation
   A: The membrane's resting potential
   (b) Point 1: Stimulus causes opening of Na^+ channels and Na^+ begins to flow into the cell.
   (c) Rapid Na^+ influx = rapid depolarisation.

Encoding Information (page 51)

1. (a) Stimulus strength is encoded by the frequency of action potentials.
   (b) Action potentials are indistinguishable from each other so amplitude modulation is not possible; information about stimulus strength must be given by frequency modulation.

2. In the Pacinian corpuscle, stronger pressures produce larger receptor potentials, which depolarise the beginning of the axon to threshold more rapidly and therefore lead to a higher frequency of action potentials. Weaker stimuli produce smaller receptor potentials which take longer, through summation, to generate an action potential.

3. Sensory adaptation allows the nervous system to ignore constant stimuli that do not change in intensity. This prevents over-stimulation and allows constant, background sensory information to be ignored.

Reflexes (page 52)

1. Higher reasoning is not a preferable feature of reflexes because it would slow down the response time. The adaptive value of reflexes is in allowing a very rapid response to a stimulus.

2. A spinal reflex involves integration within the spinal cord, e.g. knee jerk or pain withdrawal. A cranial reflex involves integration within the brain stem (e.g. pupillary light reflex).

3. (a) A monosynaptic reflex arc involves only one synapse in the CNS (e.g. knee jerk reflex), whereas a polysynaptic reflex arc involves more than one synapse within the CNS (e.g. pain withdrawal).
   (b) A monosynaptic reflex would be faster because there is synaptic delay due to the diffusion of neurotransmitter at only one junction.

4. (a) Newborn reflexes equip them with the appropriate survival behaviour in their otherwise helpless state: the rooting reflex helps them to locate a nipple, the suckling reflex ensures feeding, the startle reflex induces crying, invoking a parental care response, the grasp reflex ensures they keep contact with (usually) the mother.

(b) The presence of these reflexes indicates appropriate development. An absence of reflex behaviours in newborns may indicate neural damage or developmental impairment.

The Cholinergic Synapse (page 53)

1. A **synapse** is a junction between the end of one axon and the dendrite or cell body of a receiving neurone. **Note**: A synapse can also occur between the end of one axon and a muscle cell (neuromuscular junction).

2. Arrival of a nerve impulse at the end of the axon causes an influx of calcium. This induces the vesicles to release their neurotransmitter into the cleft.

3. Delay at the synapse is caused by the time it takes for the neurotransmitter to diffuse across the gap (synaptic cleft) between neurones.

4. (a) Neurotransmitter (NT) is degraded into component molecules by enzyme activity on the membrane of the receiving neurone (in this case, acetylcholin-esterase acts on Ach to produce acetyl and choline). This reference is to the cholinergic synapse pictured. Continued action of the NT at adrenergic synapses is prevented by reuptake of the NT (noradrenaline) by the presynaptic neurone.
   (b) The neurotransmitter must be deactivated so that it does not continue to stimulate the receiving neurone (continued stimulation would lead to depletion of neurotransmitter and fatigue of the nerve). Deactivation allows recovery of the neurone so that it can respond to further impulses.

5. Function of acetylcholine (either of):
   - It occurs at the synapse between motor neurones and muscle cells, where it causes depolarisation of the muscle cell (and leads to muscle contraction).
   - Ach is released by all parasympathetic fibres (autonomic nervous system) where it may cause an excitatory or inhibitory response (depending on the postsynaptic receptor with which it interacts). NOTE: Ach is also released by preganglionic fibres in the sympathetic division of the ANS.

6. The amount of neurotransmitter released influences the response of the receiving cell (response strength is proportional to amount of neurotransmitter released).

Integration at Synapses (page 54)

1. Integration refers to the interpretation and coordination (by the central nervous system) of inputs from many sources (inputs may be inhibitory or excitatory).

2. (a) **Summation**: The additive effect of presynaptic inputs (impulses) in the postsynaptic cell (neurone or muscle fibre).
   (b) **Spatial summation** refers to the summation of impulses from **separate** axon terminals arriving simultaneously at the postsynaptic cell. **Temporal summation** refers to the arrival of several impulses from a **single** axon terminal in rapid succession (the postsynaptic potentials are so close together in time that they can sum to generate an action potential).

3. (a) **Acetylcholine** is the NT involved; arrival of an action potential at the neuromuscular junction causes the release of Ach from the synaptic knobs.
   (b) Ach causes **depolarisation** of the postsynaptic membrane (in this case,the sarcolemma). **Note**: The depolarisation in response to the arrival of an action potential at the postsynaptic cell is essentially the same as that occurring at any excitatory synapse involving Ach neurotransmitter.

KEY TERMS: Mix and Match (page 55)

Acetylcholine (X), Action potential (R), Biological transducers (L), Cholinergic synapse (T), Electrochemical gradient (C), Motor neurone (E), Myeline (U), Myleinated neurone (P), Neuromuscular junction (H), Nuerone (A), Neurotransmitter (M), Nodes of Ranvier (V), Non-myeilnated neurone (I), Postsynaptic (D), Presynaptic (Q), Refractory period (O), Resting potential (J), Saltatory conduction (F), Schwann cells (W), Sensory neurone (K), Sensory receptor (G), Stimulus (B), Synapse (N), Synaptic integration (S).

The Endocrine System (page 57)

1. A **neurotransmitter** is a chemical messenger that is released at a chemical synapse and stimulates a post-synaptic cell. In contrast, **hormones** are chemical messengers that are released from specialised cells into the blood where they circulate and stimulate target cells. **Note**: Some hormones (e.g. adrenalin) may also function as neurotransmitters if they occur at synapses.

2. (a) Pituitary: Master gland secreting at least nine hormones, including growth hormone and TSH
   (b) Ovaries:Produce estrogen and progesterone in response to hormones from the pituitary.
   (c) Pineal gland: Secretes melatonin to regulate sleep patterns and cycles of reproductive hormones.
   (d) Parathyroid glands: The hormone from this gland regulates the levels of calcium in the blood
   (e) Thyroid: Produces hormones involved in the regulation of metabolic rate.

3. (a) **Hormonal stimulus**: Another hormone acts as the stimulus for hormone release, e.g. ACTH from the anterior pituitary stimulates the synthesis and release of glucocorticoids and mineralocorticoids from the adrenal cortex.
   (b) **Humoral stimulus**: A component in the blood acts as a stimulus for hormone release, e.g. high blood glucose stimulates release of insulin.
   (c) **Neural stimulus**: .A nerve impulse stimulates release of a hormone, e.g. sympathetic nervous stimulation of the adrenal medulla stimulates release of adrenaline.

4. (a)-(c) together below. Several examples are described. In general, blood hormone level provides the information (via negative feedback) to increase or decrease secretion. For anterior pituitary hormones, this is mediated via hypothalamic releasing factors.
   (a) Target tissue: Most tissues, especially skeletal. Hormone produced: Growth hormone (GH) (secreted by the anterior pituitary).
   (b) Homeostatic function: Stimulates protein metabolism and general growth of body cells, especially bone.
   (c) Regulation: Via releasing and inhibiting hormones from the hypothalamus. When GH levels are low, release is stimulated by growth hormone releasing hormone. When GH levels are high, release is

inhibited by growth hormone inhibiting hormone.

(a) Target tissue: Mammary glands.
Hormone produced: Prolactin (secreted by the anterior pituitary).

(b) Homeostatic function: Stimulates and maintains milk production and secretion.

(c) Regulation: Via releasing (PRH) and inhibiting (PIH) hormones from the hypothalamus. **Note**: During menstrual cycles, prolactin secretion is inhibited by hypothalamic PIH. PRH from the hypothalamus promotes prolactin release in the prepared mammary gland. Suckling reduces the output of PIH and also increases prolactin secretion.

(a) Target tissue: Liver, blood vessels, kidneys.
Hormone produced: Adrenaline (secreted by the adrenal glands).

(b) Homeostatic function: Increases blood sugar, constricts blood vessels in kidney and liver. Prepares for fight or flight.

(c) Regulation: Nervous stimulation of the adrenal glands via the hypothalamus stimulates increased secretion of adrenaline. Low blood sugar also stimulates adrenaline secretion directly.

(a) Target tissue: Kidney.
Hormone produced: Antidiuretic hormone (ADH) (secreted by the posterior pituitary).

(b) Homeostatic function: Promotes reabsorption of water and decreases urine volume.

(c) Regulation: Secretion stimulated by low blood volume (water concentration), pain, stress, anxiety, nicotine. Alcohol inhibits ADH secretion.

5. (a) Each of the adrenals comprises an inner medulla and an outer cortex. These regions are structurally and functionally distinct.
   (b) The inner medulla secretes catecholamines (adrenaline and noradrenaline). The outer cortex secretes corticosteroid hormones which regulate carbohydrate and mineral metabolism.
   (c) The anterior pituitary secretes ACTH, which regulates the secretion of corticosteroids from the adrenal cortex.
   (d) The inner medulla is essentially a modified sympathetic ganglion, which is why its secretions (catecholamines) are the same as those from sympathetic NS neurones.

The Hypothalamus and Pituitary (page 59)

1. (a) The anterior pituitary is glandular and secretes hormones in response to releasing hormones from the hypothalamus. The posterior pituitary is neural in origin and simply stores and releases neurohormones that originate in the hypothalamic neurosecretory cells.
   (b) The posterior pituitary secretes neurohormones from modified secretory neurones, whereas the anterior pituitary secretes peptide hormones when influenced by other hormonal signals.
2. Neurohormones from the hypothalamus control the release of hormones from the anterior pituitary. Neurosecretory cells in the hypothalamus also produce oxytocin and ADH, which are stored in and released from the posterior pituitary. Oxytocin has a reproductive role and ADH, is involved in regulating urine volume.
3. The thyroid and adrenals rely on hormones from the pituitary (TSH and ACTH respectively) to function properly. If secretion of these hormones stop, the glands will not be stimulated and will atrophy.
4. The hypothalamus controls hormonal secretion from the pituitary. Without its regulatory input, the pituitary would cease to function.

Signal Transduction (page 60)

1. The first messenger is the hormone or other signal molecule that binds to the membrane receptor. Some first messengers (e.g. steroids) act directly by entering the cells and directly altering gene expression. Some first messengers can act directly by binding to the membrane receptor and activating the G protein complex associated with the cytoplasmic end of the receptor. The activated G protein then brings about the cellular response. When a second messenger is involved, the first messenger (hormone) activates a G protein complex as before, but the G protein activates a second messenger (e.g. cAMP) that is responsible for a signal cascade that brings about the cellular response.
2. The binding of a hormone molecule to a receptor, initiates a series of reactions within the cell that result in, often far reaching, effects. In many cases, hormones exert their effects by influencing the enzymes associated with membranes or genetic control.
3. Both involve a specific recognition reaction. In the case of enzymes, recognition and binding to the substrate; in the case of hormones, recognition and binding to a cellular receptor.

Pancreatic Histology (page 61)

1. Within the pancreas, the endocrine portions are histologically distinct from the exocrine (digestive) portions. The endocrine tissue is located in the pancreatic islets of Langerhans and comprises several cell types which secrete into the blood five hormones, including those regulating blood glucose. The exocrine portion forms the bulk of the pancreatic tissue and consists of secretory cells organised into clusters called acini. These produce alkaline fluid and enzyme precursors, which are conveyed to the duodenum of the small intestine via the pancreatic duct.

Control of Blood Glucose (page 62)

1. (a) Stimulus: Rise in the levels of glucose in the blood above a set level (about 100 mg per 100 cm^3).
   (b) Stimulus: Fall in blood glucose levels below a set level (about 75 mg per 100 cm^3).
   (c) Glucagon brings about the production (and subsequent release) of glucose from the liver by the breakdown of glycogen and the synthesis of glucose from amino acids.
   (d) Insulin increases glucose uptake by cells (thereby lowering blood glucose) and brings about production of glycogen and fat from glucose in the liver.
2. Negative feedback mechanisms prevent excessive fluctuations in blood glucose (BG). Fall in BG triggers glucagon release, BG rises, normal BG is restored, and glucagon release stops. Rise in BG triggers insulin release, BG falls, normal BG is restored, and insulin release stops.

3. Glycogen stores in the liver become depleted and **fats** remain the next most favoured energy source available to the body. **Note**: Metabolism of fats alone for energy over an extended period of time can result in metabolic acidosis and is not recommended.

The Liver in Carbohydrate Metabolism (page 63)

1. In any order:
   (a) Glycogenesis: the production of glycogen from glucose in the liver, stimulated by insulin.
   (b) Glycogenolysis: breakdown of glycogen to produce glucose, stimulated by adrenaline and glucagon.
   (c) Gluconeogenesis: the production of glucose from non-carbohydrate sources, stimulated by adrenaline and glucocorticoid hormones.

2. (a) Process at 1: Glycogenesis (formation of glycogen from glucose).
   (b) Process at 2: Glycogenolysis (glycogen breakdown).
   (c) Process at 3: Gluconeogensis (formation of glucose from non-carbohydrate sources).

3. Interconversion of carbohydrates is essential to regulating blood glucose levels and maintaining a readily available supply of glucose as fuel without incurring the homeostatic problems of high circulating levels of glucose.

Mechanism of Insulin Secretion (page 64)

1. (a) Glucose transporter protein transports the glucose molecules into the beta cell.
   (b) Rise in intracellular ATP causes ATP-sensitive potassium channels to close.
   (c) Membrane depolarisation activates the voltage-gated Ca^{2+} channels.
   (d) Activation of the voltage-gated Ca^{2+} channels results in Ca^{2+} being transported into the beta cell. This initiates transport of insulin across the membrane into the blood.

2. An extensive network of blood vessels is required to deliver glucose efficiently to the beta cells as the trigger for insulin secretion and to transport secreted insulin from the pancreas and into the general circulation.

3. A two phase release means that the body can quickly respond to a sudden influx of glucose from a meal with very rapid cellular uptake of glucose and then follow this with a more sustained, slower release based on the rate at which the insulin is synthesised, processed and secreted. This keeps blood glucose levels more stable during the 1-2 hours immediately following a meal.

Diabetes Mellitus (page 41)

1. With a lack of insulin (or lack of response to insulin), the body's cells are unable to take up glucose from the blood and, as a result, blood glucose remains high.

2. Type 1 diabetes arises because of a complete lack of insulin (as a result of destruction of the beta cells during childhood) and is treated primarily with the regular injection of insulin to enable the body to take up and utilise glucose after meals. Type 2 diabetes is the result of insulin resistance, i.e. the cells no longer respond to insulin or respond at too low a level. Treatment is centred around controlling the factors exacerbating the diabetes: controlling weight and diet, and increasing exercise, although anti-diabetic drugs and insulin therapy may be needed in severe cases.

3. The increase in type 2 diabetes has been associated with the increasing trend towards sedentary lifestyles, and the increasing proportion of overweight and obese people in the population. This proportion is now very high (more than 50% in some cases), so much so that young people are increasingly being diagnosed with type 2 diabetes (in previous decades, it was a disease of late middle age).

4. (a) Difficulties encountered include:
   - Difficulties in promoting differentiation of the stem cells (the correct culturing environment, and the correct growth factors, delivered at the correct time, are absolutely necessary), especially if the stem cells are not ESCs.
   - Inadequate levels of insulin production, or (in transformed cells) inadequate expression of the gene once inserted.

   (b) Adult stem cells are taken from cord blood or bone marrow whereas ESCs are derived from early stage embryos, which (to date) are destroyed by the process. This causes issues of embryonic rights from those concerned with the sacrifice of a potential life.

Control of Heart Rate (page 67)

1. Myogenic means that the contractions arise as an intrinsic property of the cardiac muscle itself.

2. The sinoatrial node consists of specialised muscle cells that act as a pacemaker, setting the rhythm of the beat and initiating the cardiac cycle.

3. Noradrenaline is released from the axon terminals of the cardiac nerve (sympathetic stimulation) and acts as a neurotransmitter to increase heart rate. Noradrenaline is also released from sympathetic nerves supplying the adrenal medulla, stimulating the release of noadrenaline (and adrenaline) which act as hormones (carried in the blood) to increase cardiac output.

4. Elevated heart rate increases cardiac output, supplying more blood to muscles in preparation for responding to the stress (e.g. running or fighting).

5. (a) Cardiovascular control centre is located in the medulla oblongata (medulla) and consists of the accelerator centre and the inhibitory centre.
   (b) The accelerator centre acts to increase the rate and force of heart contraction, while the inhibitory centre acts to decrease heart rate and force of contraction.

6. (a) Increases heart rate via release of noradrenaline
   (b) Decreases heart rate via release of acetylcholine

7. (a) Increased arterial flow (in aorta and carotid arteries).
   (b) Stretch receptors in carotid sinus and aorta detect an increase in arterial flow and send afferent impulses to the inhibitory centre in the medulla. The inhibitory centre mediates a decrease in heart rate via the vagus nerve (the carotid and aortic reflexes). There is a subsequent decrease in cardiac output

and arterial blood pressure.

8. (a) and (b) any of the following in any order:
   - Aortic pressure receptors (baroreceptors) in the wall of the aortic arch respond to increased arterial blood flow in the aorta.
   - Carotid baroreceptors in the carotid sinus respond to increased arterial flow in the carotid artery.
   - Baroreceptors in the vena cava and the right atrium respond to increased venous return (mediates an increase in heart rate - the Bainbridge reflex).

8. (a) Individuals have different tolerances to the same level of a substance (also depends on their previous intakes of other substances such as coffee). Different body mass will affect the response also.
   (b) Controls should drink an energy drink that does not contain guarana.

KEY TERMS: Word Find (page 69)

X	T	M	F	X	V	T	A	D	R	E	N	A	L	G	L	A	N	D	S	D	X	P	A	E
B	H	A	H	M	P	A	U	F	I	R	S	T	M	E	S	S	E	N	G	E	R	M	Q	X
W	L	O	Y	U	K	U	X	U	G	N	O	R	A	D	R	E	N	A	L	I	N	E	C	G
S	I	G	N	A	L	T	R	A	N	S	D	U	C	T	I	O	N	P	A	T	H	W	A	Y
F	K	L	Z	X	I	S	T	E	M	C	E	L	L	T	H	E	R	A	P	Y	W	W	N	A
G	E	N	D	O	C	R	I	N	E	G	L	A	N	D	W	T	M	U	W	H	H	O	C	L
G	L	U	C	O	N	E	O	G	E	N	E	S	I	S	K	S	E	D	W	B	G	Z	C	A
Y	R	S	H	Q	G	N	T	P	A	N	C	R	E	A	S	P	D	C	Y	A	E	I	Y	Z
H	B	A	N	D	A	D	R	E	N	A	L	I	N	E	T	F	U	X	C	X	P	B	C	Q
N	A	D	R	E	N	A	L	M	E	D	U	L	L	A	T	H	L	U	B	M	H	B	L	H
W	I	H	K	U	S	D	I	A	B	E	T	E	S	M	E	L	L	I	T	U	S	V	I	O
N	N	E	X	O	C	R	I	N	E	G	L	A	N	D	M	G	A	C	L	B	P	D	C	R
Y	S	H	I	F	V	X	V	C	A	T	E	C	H	O	L	A	M	I	N	E	S	Z	A	M
X	U	Z	A	S	N	K	S	E	C	O	N	D	M	E	S	S	E	N	G	E	R	Z	M	O
K	L	C	V	S	B	O	L	B	B	G	L	Y	C	O	G	E	N	E	S	I	S	K	P	N
D	I	I	S	L	E	T	S	O	F	L	A	N	G	E	R	H	A	N	S	F	F	T	J	E
W	N	C	E	A	A	G	L	Y	C	O	G	E	N	O	L	Y	S	I	S	D	E	L	P	S

Waste Products in Humans (page 71)

1. Excretion enables the toxic by-products of metabolism (carbon dioxide, nitrogenous wastes, ions in excess of need) as well as drugs and poisons to be eliminated from the body before they can disrupt the functioning of organ systems.

2. **Carbon dioxide**: Origin: all metabolising cells. Organ of excretion: lungs.
   Water: Origin: all metabolising cells. Organs of excretion: lungs, kidneys, gut, skin.
   Bile pigments: Origin: breakdown of haemoglobin in liver. Organ of excretion: gut; the breakdown product passes out in the faeces.
   Urea: Origin: produced in the liver from ammonia (resulting after breakdown of amino and nucleic acids). Organs of excretion: kidneys, skin.
   Ions: Origin: general result of cellular metabolism. Organs of excretion: kidneys, skin, gut.
   Hormones: Origin: endocrine organs, sometimes ingested (synthetic hormones and anti-inflammatories). Organs of excretion: kidneys, skin.
   Poisons: Origin: ingested or inhaled from external sources. Organs of excretion: kidneys.
   Drugs: Origin: ingested or inhaled from external sources. Organs of excretion: kidneys.

3. The liver is responsible for the production of urea from ammonia in the ornithine cycle and also produces bile pigments from the breakdown of haemoglobin.

4. Short answer: Urea is less toxic than ammonia but still soluble enough to be transported in the body fluids.
   Further explanation: Ammonia, is highly soluble and requires little energy to produce, but it is highly toxic. Some aquatic organisms (but not aquatic mammals) can excrete it because it is diluted in the environment.

5. – Problems of fluid retention: oedema and retention of fluids containing toxins and waste products.
   – Problems of salt retention leading to hypertension and heart problems as the heart works harder to move the blood through constricted vessels.
   – Problems with the retention of ions other than sodium leading to the toxic effects of high ion levels.
   – Poisoning of the body with its own metabolic wastes eventually leads to coma and death.

The Structure of the Liver (page 72)

1. Hepatocytes

2. Portal triad comprises bile ductule, branch of the hepatic portal vein, and branch of the hepatic portal artery.

3. (a) **Vascular functions**: Any of:- manufactures heparin and blood proteins, acts as a reservoir of blood, being able to store and release blood as required to maintain blood volume.
   (b) **Metabolic functions**: Central to the metabolism of amino acids (e.g. deamination), fats (gluconeogenesis), and carbohydrates (e.g. glycogenolysis, glycogenesis). Synthesises synthesises cholesterol, stores minerals and vitamins, detoxifies poisons.
   (c) **Secretory and excretory functions**: Secretes bile, produces urea for excretion of nitrogen, excretes hormones.

Histology of the Liver (page 73)

1. (a) **Supply 1**: Branches of the hepatic artery. **Purpose**: Supply of oxygen and nutrients to the liver tissue.
   (b) **Supply 2**: Hepatic portal vein. **Purpose**: Brings nutrient-rich blood to the liver for processing by the liver cells.

2. (a) **Bile canaliculi**: Carry the bile (secreted by the hepatocytes) to the bile ductules where it then flows into the bile duct.
   (b) **Phagocytic Kupffer cells**: Engulf microbes and break down spent red blood cells.
   (c) **Central vein**: Carries blood (mix of hepatic portal and arterial blood) that has passed through the liver lobule to the hepatic vein (which exits the liver).
   (d) **Sinusoids**: Blood spaces that carry the mix of hepatic portal and arterial blood through the lobules, for processing, and supply of oxygen and nutrients.

3. Venous supply through the hepatic portal system provides a supply of nutrient-rich blood from the gut directly to the liver for processing.

4. The liver is richly vascularised with a system of capillary-like sinusoids ramifying throughout. At any one time, more than half of the 10-20% of liver's volume is in the sinusoids.

5. Sinusoids are leakier than capillaries so small and

medium sized proteins can easily leave and enter the blood. This facilitates exchanges between the blood and the hepatocytes.

The Liver's Role In Protein Metabolism (page 74)

1. **Aspects of protein metabolism** (a-c in any order):
   (a) Transamination of amino acids to create new, non-essential amino acids.
   (b) Deamination of excess amino acids and production of urea in the urea cycle.
   (c) Synthesis of plasma proteins.
2. Deamination produces keto acids, which feed into the Krebs cycle and are oxidised to yield ATP, NH_2 joins with CO_2 and enters the ornithine cycle to produce urea.
3. Symptoms would be a build up of ammonia in the tissues and, unless addressed by management of diet to minimise protein content, it would be fatal.

The Urinary System (page 75)

1. The urinary system comprises the **kidneys**, which produce urine containing the products of excretion, the **renal blood vessels**, which transfer blood to and from the kidneys, the **ureters**, which carry urine to the bladder from the kidney, the **bladder**, which stores urine before it is passed out of the body, and the **urethra**, which conducts urine from the bladder to the outside of the body.
2. 99.4%
3. In maintaining its filtration rates, the kidney requires blood at a higher pressure than other organs because large quantities of fluid must be forced through the capillaries of the glomerulus.
4. Fatty connective tissue anchors the kidneys in place and insulates and protects them from external damage.

Urine Analysis (page 76)

1. (a) Antibodies are used to detect the presence of the hormone (HCG) produced by the placenta in pregnancy. The antibodies are produced against the glycoprotein hormone and can detect it at low levels.
   (b) If the test is performed too early in the pregnancy, the levels of HCG will be too low to enable detection (placenta does not develop until 12 weeks of pregnancy).
2. (a) Anabolic steroid testing is used to detect the presence of drugs so that no competitor should have an unfair (drug) advantage over any other.
   (b) Athletes withhold drug use for a period before testing so that the body has had time to break down and metabolise the drug and excrete it (thereby avoiding detection).

The Physiology of the Kidney (page 77)

1. A nephron is a selective filtering element in the kidney. Each nephron is divided into regions where the blood is filtered, and where the filtrate is modified by secretion and reabsorption. By these processes, the nephrons produce the excretory fluid, urine.
2. (a) **Glomerular filtration**: Produces an initial filtrate of the blood that is similar in composition to blood and can be modified to produce the urine.
   (b) **Active secretion**: **Required answer**: Secretion allows the body to get rid of unwanted substances into the urine. **Extra detail**: Active secretion of chloride in the ascending limb (with sodium following passively) contributes to the maintenance of the salt gradient in the extracellular fluid (this gradient allows water to be reabsorbed in the collecting duct). Secretion of toxins and unwanted ions into the filtrate in the distal tubules allows the blood composition to be adjusted and poisons to be excreted. Energy is used to secrete these substances against their concentration gradients.
   (c) **Reabsorption**: Essential process that allows the useful substances (required by the body) to be retained from the filtrate (particularly the initial filtrate, where 90% is reabsorbed). The body would waste energy if these substances were not retained.
   (d) **Osmosis**: **Required answer**: Osmotic loss of water allows the urine to be concentrated (via loss of water). **Extra detail**: Osmosis is important in two regions of the nephron: In the descending limb of the loop of Henle, osmotic loss of water concentrates the filtrate so that salt can be withdrawn from the ascending limb to contribute to the salt gradient in the extracellular fluid. In the collecting duct, loss of water by osmosis provides the final concentration of the urine.
3. (a) The salt gradient allows water to be withdrawn from the urine (allows the urine to be concentrated). **Note**: Because the salt gradient increases through the medullary region, the osmotic gradient is maintained and water can be continually withdrawn from the urine.
   (b) Salt gradient is produced by the active and passive movement of salt from the filtrate into the extracellular fluid in the medulla.

Control of Urine Output (page 79)

1. (a) Diabetes insipidus is characterised by excretion of large amounts of very dilute urine (accompanied by a great thirst). The lack of ADH causes excessive urine production (ADH reduces urine output).
   (b) Diabetes insipidus is treated by administering ADH.
2. Alcohol inhibits ADH release causing greater urine output, resulting in dehydration and thirst.
3. (a) Aldosterone increases sodium reabsorption in the distal convoluted tubule.
   (b) Water follows the salt osmotically and the net effect is that blood volume (therefore pressure) increases.
4. Decreases or increases in blood volume are detected by hypothalamic osmoreceptors and the secretion of ADH increases or decreases accordingly. This results in an adjustment of urine output until homeostasis is restored. The adjustments made in response to the ADH release act back on the hypothalamus to counter further change. Note that, by a more complex mechanism, low blood volumes also stimulate the release of aldosterone, which induces Na^+ reabsorption

in the kidney and (by osmosis) more absorption of water and thus restoration of blood volume.

Kidney Transplants (page 80)

1. Acute renal failure arises suddenly as a result of infection, blood loss, or dehydration. ARF is characterised by a very sudden drop in urine volume. Chronic renal failure develops over months or years as a result of poorly controlled diabetes or high blood pressure, or chronic kidney disease. Unlike ARF, recovery from CRF is not possible.

2. (a) Creatinine is produced at a relatively constant rate and is usually filtered out by the kidneys, so if the levels increase in the blood it would indicate that the kidneys are not operating normally.
   (b) Creatinine clearance is a better measure of renal function than serum creatinine because it indicates early if kidneys are failing. Serum creatinine levels will only rise when kidney function is already seriously impaired.

3. Kidney transplantation (if the tissue is a good match) offers a high chance of success and a normal life away from the constraints of continual dialysis. Problems include the need to take immunosuppressant drugs and the risk that a suitable donor will not be avaiable when required. Life-time dialysis is expensive, time consuming and cannot help regulate blood pressure in the way that a kidney can. There is also a risk of infection (this is higher with peritoneal dialysis).

Renal Dialysis (page 81)

1. The dialysing solution is constantly been replaced because it needs to be free of urea and other wastes in order to maintain the concentration gradient between the blood and the dialysate. Without a gradient, urea and other wastes would stay in the blood.

2. Other ions and small molecules do not diffuse into the dialysate because they are at a similar concentration in both blood and dialysate, i.e. the dialysate has a similar ionic composition to blood and there is no concentration gradient for these molecules.

3. The urea passes into the dialysate because there is always less urea present in dialysate than in blood. Therefore there is a concentration gradient for urea between the blood and the dialysate.

4. The general transport process involved in dialysis is diffusion; the movement of molecules from a region of high concentration to a region of low concentration.

5. The dialysing solution runs in the opposite direction to that of the blood (similar to countercurrent heat exchangers) because in this way almost all of the urea can be removed from the blood in the shortest possible time. **Further explanation**: The blood at the beginning of the dialysis column (high urea) encounters dialysate that already contains some urea, but there is still a concentration gradient from blood to dialysate. By the time the blood reaches the end of the dialysis column most of the urea has been removed, but it encounters fresh dialysing solution (no urea) and there is still a concentration gradient. Having blood and dialysate running in opposite direction maintains the concentration gradient for a longer time. If the two fluids ran in the same direction the concentrations would quickly equilibrate, and urea would cease to pass into the dialysate.

6. The clot and bubble trap are necessary in order to remove small blood coagulations (clotting) and air bubbles which might form during the dialysis process. If these were allowed to enter the bloodstream they could cause stroke or embolism (blood vessel obstruction).

KEY TERMS: Mix and Match (page 82)

Anabolic steroids (G), Antidiuretic hormone (L), Collecting duct (W), Deamination (F), Detoxification (S), Distal convoluted tubule (B), Excretion (J), Glomerulus (A), Hepatocytes (Z), Hypothalamus (P), Kidney (H), Kidney failure (E), Kidney transplant (D), Liver (C), Liver lobule (T), Loop of Henle (O), Ornithine cycle (X), Osmoreceptor (AA), Proximal convoluted tubule (Y), Renal dialysis (R), Secretion (I), Selective reabsorption (M), Transamination (Q), Ultrafiltration (U), Urea (K), Urine (V), Urine analysis (N).

Plants as Producers (page 84)

1. (a) water + carbon dioxide (in the presence of light and chlorophyll) → glucose + oxygen + water
   (b) $12H_2O + 6CO_2 \rightarrow C_6H_{12}O_6 + 6O_2 + 6H_2O$

2. Importance of photosynthesis (in any order):
   (a) Transforms light energy into chemical energy available to food chains.
   (b) Creates organic molecules used as building blocks for creating more complex molecules.
   (c) Releases free oxygen into the atmosphere; required by many other life forms.

3. Algae are producers and need to remain in the euphotic zone; the zone where there is enough light penetration for photosynthesis to occur (0-30 m).

4.
   - Oxygen becomes in shorter supply.
   - Carbon dioxide levels in the atmosphere build up with fewer plants around to act as carbon sinks.
   - Climate warms progressively.

Energy in Cells (page 85)

1. Heterotrophs (strictly chemoheterotrophs) derive energy for biosynthesis from an organic energy source (other living organisms, their dead remains, or their excreted products). Photosynthetic autotrophs (photoautotrophs) derive energy for biosynthesis from light energy (e.g. sunlight, which is the inorganic energy source). Chemosynthetic autotrophs (chemoautotrophs) derive energy for biosynthesis from an inorganic chemical energy source (e.g. hydrogen sulfide gas rising from volcanic vents).

2. (a) At this depth there is no sunlight (it is filtered out after several hundred metres). Photosynthetic organisms require a source of sunlight.
   (b) Hydrogen sulfide.
   (c) They would die due to inability to respire.
   (d) Chemosynthetic autotrophs (chemoautotrophs).

Summary of Photosynthesis (page 86)

1. (a) Grana: Membranes that contain chlorophyll and are the site of the light dependent phase of photosynthesis. The biochemical process involves energy capture via photosystems I and II.
   (b) Stroma: The liquid interior of the chloroplast in which the light independent phase takes place. The biochemical process involves carbon fixation via the Calvin cycle.

2. (a) Carbon dioxide: Comes from the air (via stomata) and provides carbon and oxygen as raw materials for the production of glucose. Some oxygen molecules contribute to the production of H_2O
   (b) Oxygen: Comes from CO_2 gas (via stomata) and H_2O (via the roots and vascular system). The oxygen from the CO_2 is incorporated into glucose and H_2O. The oxygen from the water is given off as free oxygen (a waste product).
   (c) Hydrogen: Comes from water (via the roots and vascular system) obtained from the soil. This hydrogen is incorporated into glucose and H_2O. **Clarification**: Isotope studies show that the carbon and oxygen in the carbohydrate comes from CO_2, while the free oxygen comes from H_2O.

3. Scientists use isotopes to tag molecules taken up by plants and analyse the products produced as a result of photosynthesis. For example, the use of oxygen isotopes can identify the origin of the free oxygen released in photosynthesis:
   $CO_2 + 2H_2{}^{18}O \rightarrow [CH_2O] + {}^{18}O_2 + H_2O$

4. Glucose is used as the fuel for cellular respiration, or used to construct cellulose, starch, or disaccharide molecules (e.g. sucrose). Oxygen is required for aerobic respiration and water is recycled and even reused for photosynthesis.

Chloroplasts (page 87)

1. (a) Stroma (d) Granum
   (b) Stroma lamellae (e) Thylakoid
   (c) Outer membrane (f) Inner membrane

2. (a) Chlorophyll is found in the thylakoid membrane.
   (b) Chlorophyll is a membrane-bound pigment found in and around the photosystems that embedded in the membranes. Light capture by chlorophyll is linked to electron transport in the light dependent reactions.

3. The internal membranes provide a large surface area for binding chlorophyll molecules and capturing light. Membranes are stacked in such a way that they do not shade each other.

4. Chlorophyll absorbs blue and red light but reflects green light, so leaves look green to the human eye.

Pigments and Light Absorption (page 88)

1. The absorption spectrum of a pigment is that wavelength of the light spectrum absorbed by a pigment, e.g. chlorophyll absorbs red and blue light and appears green. Represented graphically, the absorption spectrum shows the relative amounts of light absorbed at different wavelengths.

2. Accessory pigments absorb light wavelengths that chlorophyll *a* cannot absorb, and they pass their energy on to chlorophyll *a*. This broadens the action spectrum over which chlorophyll *a* can fuel photosynthesis.

Light Dependent Reactions (page 89)

1. **NADP**: Carries H_2 from the light dependent phase to the light independent reactions.

2. **Chlorophyll**: These pigment molecules trap light energy and produce high energy electrons. These are used to make ATP and NADPH. The chlorophyll molecules also split water, releasing H^+ for use in the light independent reactions and liberating free O_2.

3. Light dependent (D) phase takes place in the grana (thylakoid membranes) of the chloroplast and requires light energy to proceed. The light dependent phase generates ATP and reducing power in the form of NADPH. The electrons and hydrogen ions come from the splitting of water.

4. The ATP synthesis is coupled to electron transport. When the light strikes the chlorophyll molecules, high energy electrons are released by the chlorophyll molecules. The energy lost when the electrons are passed through a series of electron carriers is used to bond a phosphate to ADP to make ATP.
   Note: ATP is generated (in photosynthesis and cellular respiration) by **chemiosmosis**. As the electron carriers pick up the electrons, protons (H^+) pass into the space inside the thylakoid, creating a high concentration of protons there. The protons return across the thylakoid membrane down a concentration gradient via the enzyme complex, ATP synthetase that synthesises the ATP (also called ATP synthase or ATPase).

5. (a) **Non-cyclic (photo)phosphorylation**: Generation of ATP using light energy during photosynthesis. The electrons lost during this process are replaced by the splitting of water.
   (b) The term non-cyclic **photo**phosphorylation is also (commonly) used because it indicates that the energy for the phosphorylation is coming from light.

6. (a) In **cyclic photophosphorylation**, the electrons lost from photosystem II are replaced by those from photosystem I rather than from the splitting of water. ATP is generated in this process, but not NADPH. **Note**: In the cell, both cyclic and non-cyclic photophosphorylation operate to different degrees in order to keep the production of NADPH and ATP balanced.
   (b) The non-cyclic path produces ATP and NADH in roughly equal quantities but the Calvin cycle uses more ATP than NADPH. The cyclic pathway of electron flow makes up the difference.

7. It shows that a complex reaction pathway is made of less complex pathways that can operate independently. These simple pathways can then be linked through common intermediates, generating complex pathways.

Light Independent Reactions (page 65)

1. (a) 6 (b) 6 (c) 12
   (d) 12 (e) 12 (f) 6
   (g) 2 (h) 1

2. RuBisCo catalyses the reaction that splits CO_2 and joins it with ribulose 1,5-bisphosphate. It fixes carbon from the atmosphere.

3. Triose phosphate (note that you may also see this referred to as glyceraldehyde-3-phosphate, GALP, G3P or PGAL)

4. $6CO_2 + 18ATP + 12\ NADPH + 12H^+$
$\rightarrow$ 1 glucose $+18ADP + 18P_i + 12\ NADP^+ + 6H_2O$

5. The Calvin cycle will cease in the dark in most plants because the light dependent reactions stop, therefore no NADPH or ATP is produced. At night, stomata also close, reducing levels of CO_2 (there will still be some CO_2 in the leaf as a waste product of respiration).

Factors Affecting Photosynthesis (page 92)

1. (a) CO_2 concentration: Photosynthetic rate increases as the CO_2 concentration increases, and then levels off.
   (b) Light intensity: Photosynthetic rate increases rapidly as the light intensity increases and then levels off.
   (c) Temperature: Increased temperature increases the photosynthetic rate, but this effect is not marked at low CO_2.

2. The photosynthetic rate is determined by the rate at which CO_2 enters the leaf. When this declines because of low atmospheric levels, so does photosynthetic rate.

3. (a) By changing only one factor at a time (either temperature or CO_2 level) it is possible to assess the effects of each one separately.
   (b) CO_2 has the greatest effect of these two variables.
   (c) At low levels of CO_2, increase in temperature has little effect (the rate of CO_2 entry into the leaf is the greatest determinant of photosynthetic rate).

4. Glasshouses are controlled environments in which the levels of light, humidity, temperature, and CO_2 can be optimised to maximise photosynthetic rate. In particular, CO_2 enrichment in an environment where transpiration losses are minimised enables maximum productivity.

5. Student's own experimental design. Possible hypothesis is that temperature will increase the rate of photosynthesis within limits (H_0 being no effect of temperature). The choice of design and plant will be up to the student but an easy one to choose is to measure the rate of oxygen (air bubble) production in a submerged aquatic macrophyte such as *Elodea*. The temperature can then be easily changed by heating or cooling the water. Things the student should make reference to and explain if necessary:
   - the control and how it was set up
   - how the dependent variable (biological response) is to be measured and how many measurements will be made
   - how the independent variable (temperature) is to be varied and the range of that variation
   - how other variables are kept constant and the value of these variables (e.g. light level)
   - how many plants at each treatment level

KEY TERMS: Mix and Match (page 93)

Accessory pigments (D), ATP (X), Autotroph (N), Carbon dioxide (V), Carotenoids (F), Chlorophyll (H), Chloroplast (A), Chromatography (Q), Cyclic phosphorylation (Z), Glycerate-3-phosphate (S), Grana (O), Heterotroph (M), Lamellae (T), Light-dependent reactions (K), NADPH (P), Non-cyclic phosphorylation (L), Photo-phosphorylation (C), Photosynthesis (W), photosynthetic pigments (U), producers (E), Ribulose bisphosphate (Y), Rubisco (R), Stroma (I), Thylakoids (J), Triose phosphate (G).

ATP in Metabolism (page 95)

1. Respiration provides the source of ATP which is required for metabolic processes.

2. (a) Mitochondria provide the environment (membrane-bound enzymes and enzymes for the Krebs cycle) within which the oxygen-requiring reactions of cellular respiration can occur.
   (b) Compartmentalisation promotes functional efficiency because specific enzyme-controlled reactions occur only in particular regions and the required enzymes are located close together in an orderly way. Enzymes are then produced only in the regions where they are required. Compartmentalisation also facilitates close control of the enzyme reaction rate because the rate of entry and exit of substrates and end-products into and out of the cell or organelle can be more easily regulated.

3. The metabolic processes that assist in thermoregulation (muscular activity, sweating etc) are energy requiring (require ATP in order to proceed), making thermoregulation an energy-expensive process.

The Role of ATP in Cells (page 96)

1. In the presence of the enzyme ATPase, ATP is hydrolysed to produce ADP plus a free phosphate, releasing energy in the process.

2. Glucose

3. Cellular respiration (strictly substrate level phosphorylation and oxidative phosphorylation).

4. Solar energy

5. Food (gaining nutrient from plants and other animals).

6. Like a rechargeable battery, the ADP/ATP system toggles between a high energy state and a low energy. The addition of a phosphate to ADP recharges the molecule so that it can be used for cellular work.

7. **PHOTOSYNTHESIS**
   Starting materials: carbon dioxide, water (as a source of hydrogens), in the presence of light and chlorophyll.
   Waste products: oxygen, water.
   Role of hydrogen carriers: NADP: Carries hydrogen between light dependent and light independent phases (where the hydrogen is incorporated into sugars).
   Role of ATP: Produced in the light dependent phase and used in the light independent phase to make sugars from carbon dioxide and hydrogen.
   Overall biological role: Uses light energy to fix carbon into organic molecules which become part of the energy available in food chains.

CELLULAR RESPIRATION

Starting materials: organic molecules (ultimately glucose), oxygen.
Waste products: carbon dioxide, water.
Role of hydrogen carriers: NAD: Carries hydrogens to the electron transport system where their transfer between carriers is coupled to ATP production.
Role of ATP: A small amount of ATP is used initially to produce pyruvate from glucose. Produced in glycolysis, Krebs cycle, and the ETS.
Overall biological role: The process by which organisms break down energy rich molecules to release energy in a usable form (ATP).

Cellular Respiration (page 97)

1. (a) Glycolysis: cytoplasm
   (b) Krebs cycle: matrix of mitochondria
   (c) Electron transport chain: cristae of mitochondria.
2. (a) Substrate-level phosphorylation: Formation of ATP by the transfer a phosphate group from a substrate (e.g. a phosphorylated 6C sugar) to ADP directly, with no involvement of an electron transport chain.
   (b) Oxidative phosphorylation: The process by which glucose is oxidised in a series of redox reactions and the energy released in the electron transfers is coupled to ATP synthesis.

Measuring Respiration (page 98)

1. (a) RQ at 20°C/48 h = 1.97 ÷ 2.82 = **0.7** (0.698)
   (b) RQ at 20°C/1 h = 2.82 ÷ 2.82 = 1. After 2 days without feeding the cricket was metabolising fats for energy. Shortly (1 hour) after feeding it was metabolising only carbohydrate (RQ = 1).
2. (a) RQ of two seedlings during early germination:

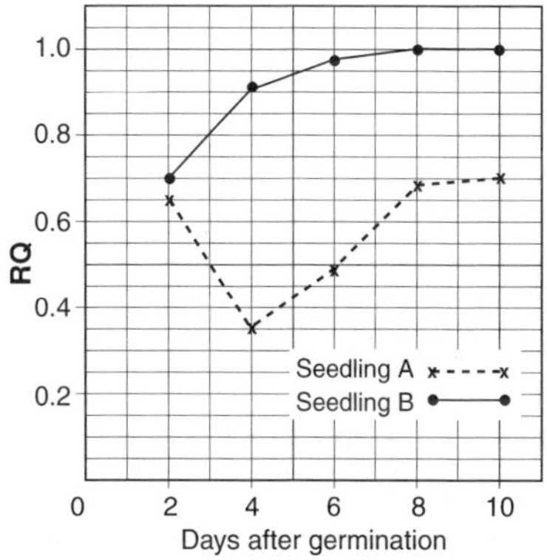

   (b) Both seedlings began their germination metabolising primarily fats for energy. However, while seedling A continued to metabolise mainly fats (with some synthesis of carbohydrate and organic acids), throughout the 10 day period, seedling B rapidly moved to metabolising carbohydrate alone. **Note**: The value of 0.91 (seedling B) may have been the result of protein metabolism alone or (more likely) respiration of a mix of fat and glucose.

The Biochemistry of Respiration (page 99)

1. (a) Glycolysis: The breakdown of glucose (a 6-C sugar) into two molecules of pyruvate (a 3-C acid called pyruvic acid) in the cytoplasm. The process is anaerobic and two molecules of ATP are generated.
   (b) Transition reaction: When oxygen is present pyruvate enters the matrix of the mitochondria and CO_2 is removed. Coenzyme A (CoA) picks up the remaining 2-C fragment of pyruvate to form acetyl coenzyme A.
   (c) Krebs cycle: The acetyl group passes into a cyclic reaction (also in the matrix) combining a 4-C molecule into a 6-C molecule and releasing the CoA for reuse. CO_2 is removed in successive steps and two molecules of ATP are generated.
   (d) Electron transport chain: Comprises a series of hydrogen and electron carriers located on the membranes of the cristae of the mitochondria. Hydrogen pairs are transferred to here from the Krebs cycle and as the hydrogens or electrons are passed along the chain they lose energy which is used to produce 34 molecules of ATP. Oxygen is the final electron acceptor and is reduced to water.
2. (a) 6 carbon atoms
   (b) 3 carbon atoms (glucose split into two)
   (c) 2 carbon atoms (1 carbon lost as CO_2)
   (d) 6 carbon atoms (2-carbon acetyl added to 4 carbon)
   (e) 5 carbon atoms (1 carbon lost as CO_2)
   (f) 4 carbon atoms (1 carbon lost as CO_2)
3. (a) Glycolysis: 2 ATPs
   (b) Krebs cycle: 2 ATPs
   (c) Electron transport chain: 34 ATPs
   (d) Total produced: 38 ATPs
4. Released as carbon dioxide (CO_2) gas and breathed out through gas exchange surfaces.
5. (a) Hydrogen atoms supply energy in the form of high energy electrons. **Note**: These are passed along the electron transport chain, losing energy as they go. The energy released is used to generate ATP.
   (b) NAD and FAD are hydrogen acceptors, transporting hydrogens to the electron transport chain.
   (c) Oxygen is the final electron acceptor at the end of the electron transport chain.
   (d) Acetyl coenzyme A, formed from pyruvate in the transition reaction, enters the Krebs cycle where CoA is released and recycled.
6. When glucose is limiting for aerobic respiration, other organic molecules e.g. fats and ultimately even protein, can provide alternative respiratory substrates.

Chemiosmosis (page 101)

1. In chemiosmosis, ATP synthesis is coupled to electron transport and movement of hydrogen ions. Energy from the passage of electrons along the chain of electron carriers is used to pump protons (H^+), against their concentration gradient, into the intermembrane space, creating a high concentration of protons there. The protons return across the membrane down a concentration gradient via the enzyme complex, ATP synthase, which synthesises the ATP.
2. Elevating the proton concentration outside the exposed inner mitochondrial membranes would result in their flowing down their concetration gradient via ATP

synthase and generating ATP.

3. A suspension of isolated chloroplasts would become alkaline because protons would be removed from the medium as ATP was generated.

4. (a) By placing chloroplasts in an acid medium, the thylakoid interior was acidified. Transfer to an alkaline medium established a proton gradient from the thylakoid interior to the medium.
   (b) The protons could flow down the concentration gradient established, via ATP synthase, and generate ATP.

Anaerobic Pathways (page 102)

1. **Aerobic respiration** requires the presence of oxygen and produces a lot of useable energy (ATP). **Fermentation** does not require oxygen and uses an alternative H^+ acceptor. There is little useable energy produced (the only ATP generated is via glycolysis)

2. Only a small amount of the energy of a glucose molecule is released in anaerobic metabolism. The remainder stays locked up in the molecule.

3. The build up of toxic products (e.g. ethanol or lactate) inhibits further metabolic activity.

KEY TERMS: Mix and Match (page 103)

Acetyl coenzyme A (C), Aerobic respiration (M), Alcoholic fermentation (V), Anaerobic respiration (B), ATP synthase (R), Cellular respiration (W), Chemiosmosis (J), Chemiosmotic theory (P), Coenzyme (D), Cristae (A), Electron acceptor (T), Electron transport chain (F), FAD (U), Glucose (E), Glycolysis (Z), Krebs cycle (S), Lactic acid fermentation (AA), Link reaction (Y), Matrix (O), Mitochondria (BB), NAD (K), Oxaloacetate (L), Oxidative phosphorylation (N), Proton gradient (X), Pyruvate (I), Respiratory substrate (Q), Substrate level phosphorylation (G), Triose phosphate (H).

The Genetic Code (page 106)

1. This exercise demonstrates the need for a 3-nucleotide sequence and the resulting degeneracy in the code.

Amino Acid	Codons						No.
Alanine	GCU	GCC	GCA	GCG			4
Arginine	CGU	CGC	CGA	CGG	AGA	AGG	6
Asparagine	AAU	AAC					2
Aspartic Acid	GAU	GAC					2
Cysteine	UGU	UGC					2
Glutamine	CAA	CAG					2
Glutamic Acid	GAA	GAG					2
Glycine	GGU	GGC	GGA	GGG			4
Histidine	CAU	CAC					2
Isoleucine	AUU	AUC	AUA				3
Leucine	UAA	UUG	CUU	CUC	CUA	CUG	6
Lysine	AAA	AAG					2
Methionine	AUG						1
Phenylalanine	UUU	UUC					2
Proline	CCU	CCC	CCA	CCG			4
Serine	UCU	UCC	UCA	UCG	AGU	AGC	6
Threonine	ACU	ACC	ACA	ACG			4
Tryptophan	UGG						1
Tyrosine	UAU	UAC					2
Valine	GUU	GUC	GUA	GUG			4

2. (a) 16 amino acids.
   (b) Two-base codons (e.g. AT, GG, CG, TC, CA) do not give enough combinations with the 4-base alphabet (A, T, G, and C) to code for the 20 amino acids.

3. Many of the codons for a single amino acid vary in the last base only. This reduces the effect of **point mutations**, resulting in new and potentially harmful amino acid sequences only in some instances.
   Note: Only 61 codons are displayed. The remaining three are 'terminator' codons ('STOP' on the mRNA table). These are 'punctuation' codons that mark the end of a gene sequence. The codon AUG (methionine) is regarded as the 'start' (initiator) codon.

The Simplest Case: Genes to Proteins (page 107)

1. The start and stop codons indicate the respective points at which the code for synthesising a polypeptide chain begins and ends.

2. (a) Template strand.
   (b) In the mRNA strand, uracil replaces thymine.

3. Transcription (to make mRNA), translation of the mRNA into a polypeptide chain, folding of polypeptide chains into the tertiary structure of the functional protein.

4. Transcription and translation occur only in 5' to 3' direction (polymerases work only 5' to 3' because the OH on the 3' is the active site for forming the phosphodiester bond).

Transcription (page 108)

1. mRNA carries a copy of the genetic instructions from the DNA in the nucleus to ribosomes in the cytoplasm. The rate of protein synthesis can be increased by making many copies of identical mRNA from the same piece of DNA.

2. (a) AUG (b) UAA, UAG, UGA

3. (a) AUG AUC GGC GCU AAA
   (b) AUG UUC GGA UAU UUU

Translation (page 109)

1. AUG AUC GGC GCU AAA

2. (a) 61
   (b) There are 64 possible codons for mRNA, but three are terminator codons. 61 codons for mRNA require 61 tRNAs each with a complementary codon.

Analysing a DNA Sample (page 110)

1. Use the mRNA table on the activity page: *The Genetic Code*, to determine the amino acid sequence.
   (a) Synthesised DNA:
   CGT AAG TAC TTG ATC AGA
   GCT CTT CGA AAA TCG
   (b) DNA sample:
   GCA TTC ATG AAC TAG TCT
   CGA GAA GCT TTT AGC

(c) mRNA:
CGU AAG UAC UUG AUC AGA
GCU CUU CGA AAA UCG
(d) Amino acids:
Arg Lys Tyr Leu Iso Arg Ala Leu Arg Lys Ser

2. (a) ATG ATC GGC GCT AAA TGT TAA
(b) ATG CGG AAT TTC CCG GCT TAG
(c) DNA replication.

3.

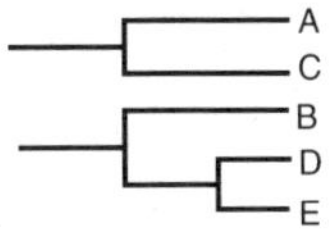

Completed dendrogram.

Protein Synthesis Summary (page 111)

1. A DNA
B Free nucleotides
C RNA polymerase enzyme
D mRNA
E Nuclear membrane
F Nuclear pore
G tRNA
H Amino acids
I Ribosome
J Polypeptide chain

2. **8** tRNA molecule is recharged with another amino acid of the same type, ready to take part in protein synthesis.
5 tRNA molecule brings in the correct amino acid to the ribosome.
1 Unwinding the DNA molecule.
3 DNA rewinds into double helix structure.
6 Anti-codon on the tRNA matches with the correct codon on the mRNA and drops off the amino acid.
7 tRNA leaves the ribosome.
4 mRNA moves through nuclear pore in the nuclear membrane to the cytoplasm.
2 mRNA synthesis: Nucleotides added to the growing strand of messenger RNA molecule.

3. The process by which the cell (and therefore the organism) manufactures proteins that may be used as building materials or controlling chemicals.

4. Ribosomal RNA (rRNA), as part of ribosomal structure. Transfer RNA (tRNA). Messenger RNA (mRNA).

5. (a)-(c) in any order:
- RNA is single stranded, DNA is double stranded.
- RNA contains the pentose sugar ribose, whereas DNA contains deoxyribose.
- DNA takes up the twisted double helix whereas RNA does not.
- RNA has had non-coding codons (introns), which were present in the DNA, removed.
- Uracil replaces thymine in the code for mRNA.
- It is mRNA that carries the message of the DNA coding strand in protein synthesis.

6. (a) Transcription (b) Translation

7. (a) UUU to UUC: This change to the third base still codes for the amino acid phenylalanine.
(b) UUU to UUA: This change to the third base changes the code for the amino acid from phenylalanine to leucine.
(c) UUU to UUA will change the protein produced.

Nature of Mutation (page 113)

1. A **beneficial** mutation confers a selective advantage in terms of fitness and a **harmful** mutation has a deleterious effect on fitness. Effects apply in the prevailing environment.

2. (a) A silent mutation changes the codon (usually the third base), but does not change the amino acid encoded by the DNA sequence.
(b) A change in the exonic sequence can disrupt RNA splicing sites or make the mRNA unstable, leading to translation errors.

3. **Somatic mutations** occur in the body (somatic) cells and are not inherited. They may affect an individual within its lifetime. **Gametic mutations** may be inherited and can therefore affect descendents.

4. Organisms such as these have short generation times, so the cumulative effects of mutations over several generations can be feasibly studied. In addition, (especially in bacteria) mutation rates are high and mutations can be induced easily.

5. The mutation does not extend to the seeds (the gametic portion which will be inherited).

Gene Mutations (page 115)

1. A **reading frame shift** occurs when the sequence of bases is offset by one position (by adding or deleting a base). This alters the order in which the bases are grouped as triplets and can severely alter the amino acid sequence.

2. (a) Reading frame shifts and nonsense substitutions.
(b) They may cause large scale disruption of the coded instructions for making a protein. Either a completely wrong amino acid sequence for part of the protein or a protein that is partly completed (missing amino acids due to an out-of-place terminator codon).

3. Because a reading frame shift severely affects the basic construction of a protein as a set sequence of amino acids, it is unlikely that the protein will be able to carry out its designated role (structural, catalytic, transport). It will lose it biological activity (functionality).

Inherited Metabolic Disorders (page 117)

1. (b) *Gene name*: HBB *Chromosome*: 11
Mutation type: autosomal recessive. *May be caused by base deletion, base insertion, or gene deletion (severity depends on the mutation).
(c) *Gene name*: CFTR *Chromosome*: 7
Mutation type: autosomal recessive. Great range: deletion, missense, nonsense, misplaced terminator codon. Most common is a deletion of 3 nucleotides.
(d) *Gene name*: IT15 *Chromosome*: 4
Mutation type: autosomal dominant. Duplication (CAG repeats of varying length).

2. Few or no haemoglobin β chains causes severe anaemia. Frequent blood transfusions are required and this can cause iron accumulation in tissues and organs.

3. Mutations would have arisen in an individual and

spread out gradually from that origin. Thus certain genetic disorders tend to have a higher occurrence in certain regions, especially where the population tends to have stayed relatively isolated geographically.

Sickle Cell Mutation (page 118)

1. (a) Bases: 21
   (b) Triplets: 7
   (c) Amino acids coded for: 7
2. mRNA: GUG CAC CUG ACU CCU GAG GAG
3. Amino acids: Val His Leu Thr Pro Glu Glu
4. Mutant DNA: CAC GTG GAC TGA GGA CAC CTC
   Type of mutation: Substitution
5. Mutant mRNA:
   GUG CAC CUG ACU CCU GUG GAG
6. Amino acids coded by mutant DNA:
   Val His Leu Thr Pro Val Glu
7. A base substitution causes one amino acid to change in the haemoglobin molecule. This makes the haemoglobin less soluble, and it deforms the red blood cells and results in many circulatory problems.

Cystic Fibrosis Mutation (page 119)

1. (a) mRNA: GGC ACC AUU AAA GAA AAU AUC AUC UUU GGU GGU
   (b) Amino acids: Gly Thr Iso Lys Glu Asn Iso Iso Phe Gly Gly
2. (a) Mutant mRNA: GGC ACC AUU AAA GAA AAU AUC AUC | GGU GGU
   (b) Type of mutation: Triplet deletion.
   (c) Amino acids coded by mutant DNA: Gly Thr Iso Lys Glu Asn Iso Iso | Gly Gly
   (d) Amino acid missing: Phenylalanine (Phe).
3. CF has varying degrees of severity because there are more than 500 mutations of the CF gene. The resulting mutant CFTR protein may not function at all, or it may function only in part, producing a system that is variously effective.

Protein Activation by Cyclic AMP (page 120)

1. Protein kinase A is a tetramer (it has four subunits). It has two regulatory subunits and two catalytic subunits.
2. cAMP binds to the regulatory subunits of protein kinase A, causing a conformational (structural) change of the protein. The change in structure results in the dissociation of the catalytic subunits from the regulatory subunits. The free catalytic subunits are enzymatically active and can phosphorylate serine residues on target proteins.
3. The catalytic subunits of protein kinase A regulate other proteins by phosphorylating their serine residues. This results in some sort of functional change to the target protein (e.g. change in enzyme activity, cellular location, or association with other proteins).

Gene Control in Prokaryotes (page 121)

1. (a) **Operon**: Consists of at least one structural gene coding for the primary enzyme structure, and two regulatory elements: the operator and the promoter.
   (b) **Regulator gene**: (repressor gene) produces a repressor substance that binds to the operator, preventing transcription of the structural genes.
   (c) **Operator**: This is a non-coding sequence of DNA that is the binding site for the repressor molecule.
   (d) **Promoter**: Site of RNA polymerase binding to start the transcription process.
   (e) **Structural genes**: Genes responsible for producing enzymes that control the metabolic pathway.
2. (a) In an inducible enzyme system, the enzymes required for the metabolism of a particular substrate are produced only when the substrate is present. This saves the cell valuable energy in not producing enzymes that have no immediate use.
   (b) Inducible enzyme systems are not adaptive when the substrate is present all (or most) of the time.
   (c) Regulation of a non-inducible system is achieved (in prokaryotes) through **gene repression**: the structural genes are normally transcribed all the time and, when the end product (e.g. tryptophan in *E. coli*) is present in excess to requirements, the genes are switched off.
3. The operon model explains diauxic growth because it links the growth phase to utilisation of different substrates. The initial growth is associated with the preferred substrate, glucose, which does not require induction, there is a lag when glucose is depleted and the genes for lactose utilisation are induced, and a second phase of growth on lactose.

Genes and the Control of Development (page 123)

1. Homeobox gene sequences make up a genetic tool kit for animal development. These genes act as genetic switches (transcription factors), turning other genes on or off in the course of development. For example, the *Hox* genes determine the positioning of body parts in organisms as diverse as *Drosophila* and mice.
2. (a) The same genes are present in essentially all taxa, and they have not changed much during their evolutionary history.
   (b) Homeobox sequences must be fundamentally important to the development of the organism. Mutations are likely to have a profound and deleterious effect on morphology or functionality so the sequences tend to remain static (i.e. mutations when they occur are fatal and not passed on).
3. The occurrence of Hox genes in clusters indicates that it is important that the genes are linked and inherited together as a unit; disruption by crossing over and recombination would not be adaptive.
4. Changes in gene expression can bring about changes in morphology, e.g. in differences in neck length in vertebrates and eyespot development on butterfly wings. Neck length is controlled by the expression of the *Hox c6* gene and where it is expressed marks the boundary between neck and trunk vertebrae. For example, in snakes the boundary is shifted forward to the base of the skull with no neck results, while in

geese the boundary is shifted backwards and a long neck results. Similarly, the development of eyespots on the wings of butterflies is controlled by switches in the *Distal-less* gene, whose expression results in a range of spots from virtually all eyespot elements expressed to very few.

Apoptosis: Programmed Cell Death (page 125)

1. Syndactyly arises when the rate of apoptosis in the developing limb has been too low to remove the tissue between the digits before the close of the developmental sequence (hence the lack of differentiation between the two toes, which remain partly joined).
2. Any one of the reasons from the following explanation: Apoptosis is a carefully regulated process, which occurs in response to particular signalling factors. Necrosis, in contrast, is the result of traumatic damage. Apoptosis results in membrane-bound cell fragments whereas necrosis results in lysing and spillage of cell contents. Apoptosis results in cell shrinkage and contraction of the chromatin, which does not occur in necrosis.
3. Roles of apoptosis, (a) and (b) any two of the following:
   - Resorption of the larval tail during amphibian metamorphosis.
   - Sloughing of the endometrium during menstruation.
   - The formation of the proper connections (synapses) between neurones in the brain (this requires that surplus cells be eliminated by apoptosis).
   - Controlled removal of virus-infected cells.
   - Controlled removal of cancerous cells.

KEY TERMS: Mix and Match (page 126)

Anticodons (T), Apoptosis (E), Beneficial mutation (G), Coding strand (A), Codon (F), Cyclic AMP (N), Exon (B), gene expression (P), Gene induction (Q), Genetic code (J), Harmful mutation (W), Homeobox sequence (O), Intron (Z), Lac operon (C), messenger RNA (H), Mutagen (BB), Mutation (V), Neutral mutation (K), Polypeptide (AA), Redundancy (X), Ribosome (S), RNA polymerase (M), Second messenger (CC), Silent mutation (R), Start codon (L), Stop codon (I), Template strand (U), transcription (DD), Transfer RNA (D), Translation (Y).

Alleles (page 128)

1. (a) Heterozygous: Each of the homologous chromosomes contains a **different** allele for the gene (one dominant and one recessive).
   (b) Homozygous dominant: Each of the homologous chromosomes contains an identical dominant allele.
   (c) Homozygous recessive: Each of the homologous chromosomes contains an identical recessive allele.
2. (a) **Aa** (b) **AA** (c) **aa**
3. Each chromosome of a **homologous pair** comes from a different parent: one of maternal origin, one of paternal origin (they originated from the egg and the sperm that formed the zygote). They contain the same sequence of genes for the same traits, but the versions of the genes (alleles) on each chromosome may differ.
4. **Alleles** are different versions of the same gene that code for the same trait. Different alleles provide phenotypic variation for the expression of a gene. There are often two alleles for a gene, one dominant and one recessive. In this case, the dominant allele will be expressed in the phenotype. Sometimes alleles for a gene can be equally dominant, in which case, both alleles will be expressed in the phenotype. Where three or more alleles for a gene exist (multiple alleles), there is more phenotypic variation in the population (for that trait) than would be the case with just two alleles.

Sources of Variation (page 129)

1. The environment can alter the phenotype by altering the basic expression of a trait. Examples include: trees that are grown at high altitude are stunted in growth, trees exposed to a strong prevailing wind appear distorted in shape (windswept), poor nutrition in infancy can retard brain and bone development.
2. Variation is the raw material on which natural selection acts. Selection acts on the phenotype (being the result of genotype and environment). Selection acts for or against particular allele combinations, enhancing or reducing the representation of these in the next generation. Selection therefore sorts the variability in a gene pool and establishes adaptive genotypes.

Mitosis vs Meiosis (page 130)

1. Mitosis involves a division of the chromatids into two new daughter cells thus maintaining the original number of chromosomes in the parent cell. Meiosis involves a division of the homologous chromosome pairs into two intermediary daughter cells thus reducing the diploid number by half. The second stage of meiosis is similar to a mitotic division, but the haploid number is maintained because the chromatids separate.
2. Recombination and independent assortment during meiosis introduce genetic diversity. Mitosis only produces daughter cells identical to the parent cell.
3. The first meiotic division is a reduction division, halving the number of chromosomes. The second division is a 'mitotic' type division, the chromatids are separated but the number of chromosomes remain the same.

Meiosis (page 131)

1. In meiosis I, homologous chromosomes pair to form bivalents. Segments of chromosome may be exchanged in crossing over and the homologues then separate. This division reduces the number of chromosomes in the intermediate cells, so that only one chromosome from each homologous pair is present.
2. In the second division of meiosis, chromatids separate (are pulled apart), but the number of chromosomes stays the same. This is more or less a 'mitotic' division.
3. Mitosis involves a division of the chromatids into two new daughter cells thus maintaining the original number of chromosomes in the parent cell. Meiosis involves a division of the homologous pairs of chromosomes into two intermediary daughter cells thus reducing the diploid number by half. Meiosis II is similar to a mitotic division, but the haploid number is maintained because the chromatids separate.

4. **A** shows metaphase of meiosis I; the homologous pairs of chromosomes are lined up on the cell equator. **B** shows metaphase of meiosis II; the individual chromatids are about to separate.

Crossing Over (page 133)

1. Unexpected combinations of alleles for genes will occur in the gametes.
2. This provides a source of increased genetic variation amongst individuals in a population; important as the raw material on which natural selection acts.

Crossing Over Problems (page 134)

Each problem stands alone (they are not a sequence).

1. (a) Gene sequences after crossing over at point 2:

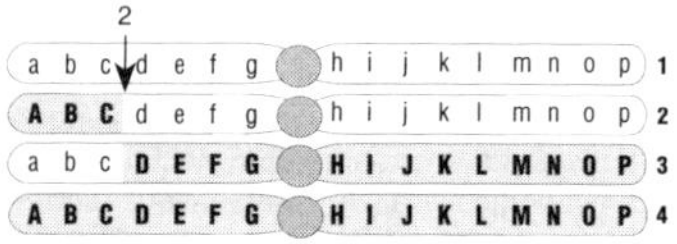

(b) A, B and C

2. (a) Gene sequences after crossing over between crossover points 6 and 7.

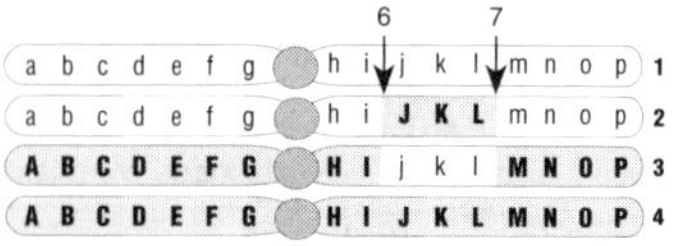

(b) J, K and L

3. (a) Gene sequences after crossing over between points 1 and 3, and 5 and 7. (Note that results for chromatids 2 and 3 are interchangeable).

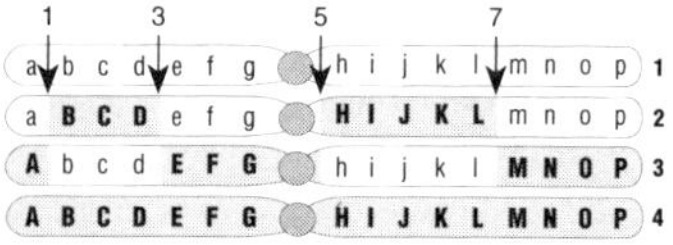

(b) B, C, D and H, I, J, K, L

4. **Crossing over** increases the number of new allele combinations in the offspring and therefore increases genetic variation in the gene pool. Crossing over counteracts the conservative effect of gene linkage.

Linkage (page 135)

1. **Linkage** refers to the situation where genes are located on the same chromosome. As a result, they tend to be inherited together as a unit.
2. (a) AaBb, Aabb, aaBb, aabb
   (b) F_1 genotype: All CucuEbeb (heterozygotes)
   F_1 phenotype: All wild type (straight wing, grey body)
3. Gene linkage reduces the amount of variation because the linked genes are inherited together and fewer genetic combinations of their alleles are possible.

Recombination (page 136)

1. **Recombination** refers to the exchange of alleles between homologous chromosomes as a result of crossing over. It produces new associations of alleles in the offspring.
2. Recombination increases the amount of genetic variation because parental linkage groups separate and new associations of alleles are formed in the offspring. The offspring show new combinations of characters that are unlike the parental types.
3. A greater than 50% recombination frequency indicates that there is independent assortment (the genes must be on separate chromosomes).

Basic Genetic Crosses (page 137)

1.

	YR	Yr	yR	yr
YR	YYRR	YYRr	YyRR	YyRr
Yr	YYRr	YYrr	YyRr	Yyrr
yR	YyRR	YyRr	yyRR	yyRr
yr	YyRr	Yyrr	yyRr	yyrr

2. Yellow-round: 9/16 Yellow-wrinkled: 3/16
   Green-round: 3/16 Green-wrinkled: 1/16
3. Ratio: 9 : 3 : 3 : 1
4. **Cross No. 1:**

(a)

M \ F	BL	Bl	bL	bl
bL	BbLL	BbLl	bbLL	bbLl
bL	BbLL	BbLl	bbLL	bbLl
bl	BbLl	Bbll	bbLl	bbll
bl	BbLl	Bbll	bbLl	bbll

(b) Genotypes: BbLL 2 bbLl 4
BbLl 4 Bbll 2
bbLL 2 bbll 2

(c) Phenotypes: 6 black/short 6 white/short
2 black/long 2 white/long

5. **Cross No. 2:**

(a) Gametes: White parent: all bL
Black parent: Bl, Bl, bl, bl

(b)

M \ F	bl	bl	bl	bl
bL	BbLL	BbLl	bbLL	bbLl
bL	BbLL	BbLl	bbLL	bbLl
bl	BbLl	Bbll	bbLl	bbll
bl	BbLl	Bbll	bbLl	bbll

(c) Genotypes: BbLl 8 bbLl 8
(d) Phenotypes: 8 black/short 8 white/short

The Test Cross (page 139)

1. To perform the test cross here you would have to cross the male with a female (brown eye, ebony body) homozygous recessive for both genes (bbee).

   Extra information:

   Depending on the male's genotype the outcomes of the test cross would produce offspring that were:
   - All wild type (brown body red eye)
   - Half wild type, and half red eye, ebony body
   - Half wild type, and half brown eye, brown body
   - 25% wild type, 25% red eye ebony, 25% brown eye, brown body, and 25% brown eye, ebony.

   Students may choose to present this information in Punnett squares.

Male gametes

Female gametes

	BE
eb	BbEe
	red eye, brown body

	BE	Be
eb	BbEe	Bbee
	red eye, brown body	red eye, ebony body

	BE	bE
eb	BbEe	bbEe
	red eye, brown body	brown eye, brown body

	BE	Be	bE	be
eb	BbEe	Bbee	bbEe	bbee
	red eye, brown body	red eye, ebony body	brown eye, brown body	brown eye, ebony body

2. A wild type male (brown or normal body and red eyes) could have one of four genotypes: BEBE, BEbE, BEBe, or BEbe

3. (a) 50% are wild type and 50% are red eye, ebony so the male must BEBe.
   (b) This is the only genotype that produces this ratio of phenotypes in the offspring (as per the second Punnett square above)

Codominance (page 140)

1. Codominant alleles are equally dominant and are fully expressed. This means that heterozygotes will have a phenotype that is different from the two homozygous genotypes.

2. (a) Diagram labels:

	White bull	Roan cow
Parent genotype:	C^WC^W	C^RC^W
Gametes:	C^W, C^W	C^R, C^W
Calf genotypes:	C^RC^W, C^WC^W ,C^RC^W, C^WC^W	
Phenotypes:	roan, white, roan, white	

   (b) Phenotype ratio: 1 : 1, roan : white (50% roan, 50% white)
   (c) By breeding only from the roan calves. Initial offspring from roan parents should include all phenotypes: white, roan, and red. By selecting only the red offspring from this generation it would be possible to breed a pure herd of red cattle.

3. (a) Diagram labels:

	Unknown bull	Roan cow
Parent genotype:	C^RC^R	C^RC^W
Gametes:	C^R, C^R	C^R, C^W
Calf genotypes:	C^RC^R, C^RC^W ,C^RC^R, C^RC^W	
Phenotypes:	red, roan, red, roan	

   (b) Unknown bull: red bull

Codominance in Multiple Allele Systems (page 141)

1. Blood group table:

Blood group **B**	BB, BO
Blood group **AB**	AB

2.

Cross 2	**Group O**	**Group O**
Gametes:	O, O	O, O
Children's genotypes:	OO, OO	OO, OO
Blood groups:	O, O	O, O
Cross 3	**Group AB**	**Group A**
Gametes:	A, B	A, O
Children's genotypes:	AA, AO	BA, BO
Blood groups:	A, A	AB, B
Cross 4	**Group A**	**Group B**
Gametes:	A, A	B, O
Children's genotypes:	AB, AO	AB, AO
Blood groups:	AB, A	AB, A
Cross 5	**Group A**	**Group O**
Gametes:	A, O	O, O
Children's genotypes:	AO, AO	OO, OO
Blood groups:	A, A	O, O
Cross 6	**Group B**	**Group O**
Gametes:	B, O	O, O
Children's genotypes:	BO, BO	OO, OO
Blood groups:	B, B	O, O

Note: Answers can be arranged differently depending on which gamete circle each allele symbol is placed. There are many more crossover combinations possible.

3. (a) Parent genotypes:

Parent genotype:	AO	OO
Gametes:	A, O	O, O
Children's genotypes:	AO, AO	OO, OO
Blood groups:	A, A	O, O

(b) 50% (0.5) (c) 50% (0.5) (d) 0% (0)

4. (a) Possible parent genotypes: Mother assumed to be heterozygous to get maximum variation in gametes (homozygous would also work).

Phenotypes	**Group A**	**Group O**
Genotypes:	AO	OO
Gametes:	A, O	O, O

Child's genotype would have to be AO or OO

(b) Therefore the only possible offspring from this couple would have been children with group **A** or group **O**. The man making the claim could not have been the father of the child.

5. (a) **A** or **B** (b) **AB, A, B** or **O**

Sex Linkage (page 143)

1.

Parent genotype:	X_oX_o	X_OY
Gametes:	X_o, X_o	X_O, Y
Kitten genotypes:	X_OX_o, X_oY	X_OX_o, X_oY
	Genotypes	**Phenotypes**
Male kittens:	X_oY	Black
Female kittens:	X_OX_o	Tortoiseshell

2.

Parent genotype:	X_oX_O	X_OY
Gametes:	X_o, X_O	X_O, Y
Kitten genotypes:	X_OX_O, X_OX_o	X_oY, X_OY
Phenotypes:	Orange female, Tortoise female	Black male, Orange male

(a) Father's genotype: X_OY
(b) Father's phenotype: Orange

3.

Parent genotype:	X_oX_o	X_OY
Gametes:	X_o, X_o	X_O, Y
Kitten genotypes:	X_OX_o, X_oY	X_OX_o, X_oY
Phenotypes:	Tortoise female, Black male	Tortoise female, Black male

(a) Father's genotype: X_OY
(b) Father's phenotype: Orange
(c) Yes, the same male cat could have fathered both litters.

4.

Parent:	Normal wife	Affected husband
Parent genotype:	XX	X_RY
Gametes:	X, X	X_R, Y
Child genotypes:	X_RX, XY	X_RX, XY
Phenotypes:	Affected girl, Normal boy	Affected girl, Normal boy

(a) Probability of having affected children = 50% or 0.5
(b) Probability of having an affected girl = 50% or 0.5
However, all girls born will be affected = 100%
(c) Probability of having an affected boy = 0% or none

5.

Parent:	Affected wife	Normal husband
Parent genotype:	X_RX	XY
Gametes:	X_R, X	X, Y
Child genotypes:	X_RX, X_RY	XX, XY
Phenotypes:	Affected girl, Affected boy	Normal girl, Normal boy

Note: Because the wife had a normal father, she must be heterozygous since her father was able to donate only an X-chromosome with the normal condition.

(a) Probability of having affected children = 50% or 0.5
(b) Probability of having an affected girl = 25% or 0.25
However, half of all girls born may be affected
(c) Probability of having an affected boy = 25% or 0.25
However, half of all boys born may be affected.

Background information for question 6: Sex linkage refers to the location of genes on one or other of the sex chromosomes (usually the X chromosome; but a few are carried on the Y). Such genes produce an inheritance pattern which is different from that shown by autosomes:
- Reciprocal crosses produce different results (unlike autosomal genes that produce the same results).
- Males carry only one allele of each gene.
- Dominance operates in females only.
- A 'cross-cross' inheritance pattern is produced: father to daughter to grandson, etc.

6. **Sex linkage** (in humans, this usually means X-linkage) is involved in a number of genetic disorders. X-linked disorders are commonly seen only in males, because they have only one locus for the gene and must express the trait. If the sex linked trait is due to a recessive allele, females will express the phenotype only when homozygous recessive. It is possible for females to inherit a double dose of the recessive allele (e.g. a colour blind daughter can be born to a colour blind father and mother who is a carrier), but this is much less likely than in males because sex linked traits are relatively uncommon. Over a hundred X-linked genes are known, including those that control:
- Blood clotting: A recessive allele for this gene causes haemophilia. It affects about 0.01% of males but is almost unheard of in females.
- Normal colour vision: A recessive allele causes red-green colour blindness affecting 8% of males but only 0.7% of females.
- Antidiuretic hormone production: A version of this gene causes some forms of diabetes insipidus.
- Muscle development: A rare recessive allele causes Duchene muscular dystrophy.

Inheritance Patterns (page 145)

1. **Autosomal recessive:**

(a)

	P	*p*
P	*PP*	*Pp*
p	*Pp*	*pp*

Male parent phenotype: Normal, carrier
Female parent phenotype: Normal, carrier

(b) Phenotype ratio: Normal 3 Albino 1

2. **Autosomal dominant:**

(a)

	W	*w*
W	*WW*	*Ww*
w	*Ww*	*ww*

Male parent phenotype: Woolly hair
Female parent phenotype: Woolly hair

(b) Phenotype ratio: Normal 1 Woolly 3

3. **Sex linked recessive:**

(a)

	X	X_h
X	XX	XX_h
Y	XY	X_hY

Male parent phenotype: Normal
Female parent phenotype: Normal, carrier

(b) Phenotype ratio:

Females:		**Males:**	
Normal	2	Normal	1
Haemophiliac	0	Haemophiliac	1

4. **Sex linked dominant:**

(a)

	X_R	X
X_R	X_RX_R	XX_R
Y	X_RY	XY

Male parent phenotype: Affected (with rickets)
Female parent phenotype: Affected (with rickets)

(b) Phenotype ratio:

Females:		**Males:**	
Normal	0	Normal	1
Rickets	2	Rickets	1

Gene Interactions (page 146)

1. **Polygeny** refers to the determination of a single trait (e.g. skin colour) by two or more genes. In contrast, **pleiotropy** is the situation where one gene affects several traits. Examples include the sickle cell mutation, which has pleiotropic effects because a large number of traits are influenced by the possession of mutant haemoglobin, and PKU which has pleiotropic effects because of the effects of accumulated phenylalanine and its derivative phenylpyruvate.
2. **Epistasis** describes the situation where one gene masks or alters the expression of other genes. In contrast, a pleiotropic gene has multiple phenotypic effects but does not alter the expression of other genes. Male pattern baldness is an example of epistasis: if expressed, baldness overrides the expression of genes determining hairline (e.g. widow's peak).
3. If a genotype is homozygous recessive for albinism, the expression of that gene (i.e no melanin produced) is epistatic to all other genes for colour.

Epistasis (page 147)

1. No. of phenotypes: 3
2. Black: B_C_ (a dominant allele for each gene)
Brown: A dominant allele for gene C only (e.g. Ccbb)
Albino: No dominant allele for gene C (e.g. ccBB, ccbb)
3.

Eggs \ Sperm	BC	Bc	bC	bc
BC	**BBCC** Black	**BBCc** Black	**BbCC** Black	**BbCc** Black
Bc	**BBCc** Black	**BBcc** Albino	**BbCc** Black	**Bbcc** Albino
bC	**BbCC** Black	**BbCc** Black	**bbCC** Brown	**bbCc** Brown
bc	**BbCc** Black	**Bbcc** Albino	**bbCc** Brown	**bbcc** Albino

Ratio: Black: brown: albino
9: 3: 4

4. Homozygous albino (bbcc) x homozygous black (BBCC):
Offspring genotype: 100% BbCc
Offspring phenotype: 100% black
5. Homozygous brown (bbCC) x homozygous black (BBCC):
Offspring genotype: 100% BbCC
Offspring phenotype: 100% black
6. Four
7. **Black**: dominant E and dominant B alleles.
Brown: dominant E, recessive bb.
Yellow with brown nose: only eebb.
Yellow with black nose: recessive ee and dominant B.
8. (a) EEBB x eebb.
All offspring will be black with genotype EeBb

(b) 1 : 1: 1: 1 ratio of:
EeBb black,
Eebb brown,
eeBb yellow with black nose
eebb yellow with brown nose
Working: A full Punnett square is not required as the backcross parent produces only gametes eb .

F \ M	EB	Eb	eB	eb
eb	EeBb	Eebb	eeBb	eebb

9. Chocolate parent must be EEbb (true-breeding). Genotype Eebb would produce half yellow offspring.
10. (a) True-breeding chocolate genotype is EEbb. Black phenotypes can be EEBB, EeBB, EEBb, or EeBb. The black parent must be heterozygous for the B allele because otherwise all offspring will be black. Therefore the black parent could be EeBb or EEBb. Either would give 50% chocolate offspring.
(b) In both cases, the other 50% of offspring are black.

11. An epistatic gene overrides the expression of genes at another locus. Dominance describes an interaction between alleles at the same gene locus. In expression of the phenotype, the epistatic allelic condition (e.g. homozygous recessive for the albino gene) overrides all other gene information, regardless of the dominance status of those genes. In simple dominance, a dominant allele will produce the corresponding phenotype.

Polygenes (page 149)

1. Punnett square

Gametes	ABC	ABc	AbC	Abc	aBC	aBc	abC	abc
ABC	AABBCC	AABBCc	AABbCC	AABbCc	AaBBCC	AaBBCc	AaBbCC	AaBbCc
ABc	AABBCc	AABBcc	AABbCc	AABbcc	AaBBCc	AaBBcc	AaBbCc	AaBbcc
AbC	AABbCC	AABbCc	AAbbCC	AAbbCc	AaBbCC	AaBbCc	AabbCC	AabbCc
Abc	AABbCc	AABbcc	AAbbCc	AAbbcc	AaBbCc	AaBbcc	AabbCc	Aabbcc
aBC	AaBBCC	AaBBCc	AaBbCC	AaBbCc	aaBBCC	aaBBCc	aaBbCC	aaBbCc
aBc	AaBBCc	AaBBcc	AaBbCc	AaBbcc	aaBBCc	aaBBcc	aaBbCc	aaBbcc
abC	AaBbCC	AaBbCc	AabbCC	AabbCc	aaBbCC	aaBbCc	aabbCC	aabbCc
abc	AaBbCc	AaBbcc	AabbCc	Aabbcc	aaBbCc	aaBbcc	aabbCc	aabbcc

Darker skin Same Lighter skin

(a) 20 (b) 27

2. Environmental influences will alter the color of a person skin (such as tanning) to different extents.

3. Traits with **continuous variation** show a normal distribution curve when sampled and a graded variation in phenotype in the population. Such phenotypes are usually determined by a large number of genes and/or environmental influence. Examples include height, weight, hand span, foot size. In contrast, traits with **discontinuous variation** fall into one of a limited number of phenotypic variants and do not show a normal distribution curve when sampled. Differences in the phenotypes of individuals in a population are marked and do not grade into each other. Such phenotypes are usually controlled by a few different alleles at a few genes. Examples include ear lobe shape and tongue roll.

4. Student's own plot. Shape of the distribution is dependent on the data collected. The plot should show a **statistically normal distribution** if sample is representative of the population and large enough.
   (a) Calculations based on the student's own data.
   (b) Continuous distribution, normal distribution, or bell shaped curve are all acceptable answers if the data conform to this pattern.
   (c) Polygenic inheritance: Several (two or more) genes are involved in determining the phenotypic trait. Environment may also have an influence, especially if traits such as weight are chosen.
   (d) A large enough sample size (30+) provides sufficient data to indicate the distribution. The larger the sample size, the more closely one would expect the data plot to approximate the normal curve (assuming the sample was drawn from a population with a normal distribution for that attribute).

Problems in Mendelian Genetics (page 151)

1. (a) They have an albino child (aa) as well as unaffected ones (AA or Aa), so the parents must both be Aa. Note: There is a 75% chance that any child of theirs will be albino.
   (b) The family are all aa.
   (c) The albino father must be aa. The mother must be Aa. The three unaffected children are Aa. Note: There is a 50% chance that any child of theirs will be albino. The observed 3:1 ratio is not surprising, given the small number of offspring.

2. (a) A pair of codominant sex-linked alleles,
   e.g. Xo = Non-red (black coat colour)
   XO = Red (orange coat colour).
   (b) Black female: XoXo Black male: XoY
   Orange female: XOXO Orange male: XOY
   Tortoiseshell female: XOXo
   Parents: XOXO x XoY
   Phenotypes of F_1: All males are orange, all females are tortoiseshell.
   (c) Parents: XoXo x XOY
   Phenotypes of F1: All males are black, all females are tortoise-shell.
   (d) Parents: Tortoise-shell female, black male.
   (e) Parents: Tortoise-shell female, orange male.

3. (a) Black: B_E_
   Golden: _ _ee
   Chocolate: bbE_
   (b) Genotype: BbEe, phenotype: All black
   (c)

Sperm (columns), Eggs (rows)

Eggs \ Sperm	EB	Eb	eB	eb
EB	EEBB Black	EEBb Black	EeBB Black	EeBb Black
Eb	EEBb Black	EEbb Choc	EeBb Black	Eebb Choc
eB	EeBB Black	EeBb Black	eeBB Yellow w/ black	eeBb Yellow w/ black
eb	EeBb Black	Eebb Choc	eeBb Yellow w/ black	eebb Yellow w/ brown

   (d) 9/16 B_E_ = 9/16 Black
   3/16 bbE_ = 3/16 Chocolate
   4/16 _ _ ee = 4/16 Yellow
   Ratio: 9 Black : 3 Chocolate : 4 Yellow.
   (e) Epistasis (ee will be yellow regardless of what allele they have for melanin production).

4. The case could be argued thus:
   – The genotypes of couple #1 must be XHX– and XHY because neither is affected. their son is affected XhY.
   – If the mother in couple #1 is XHXH there is no way they could have an affected XhY son. If the mother is a carrier XhXh, then there is a 50% chance that her son will be affected.
   – The genotypes of couple #2 must be XHX– and

XhY and their son is XHY
- The father did not pass an X chromosome to his son, so his genotype is irrelevant.
- If the mother is XHXH, all of her sons will be XHY, but if she is XHXh, then there is a 50% chance that her sons will be XhY (as for couple #1).
- Either the hospital or the parents could be correct. The answer depends on the genotype of the mothers.

5. All the males (of both generations) have spotted dorsal fins and all of the females are unspotted.
6. (a) This is called pleiotropy; a gene interaction where a single gene, through its expression, has multiple phenotypic effects.
   (b) Other examples include:
   - The disease PKU, where phenylalanine is not metabolised correctly and this affects mental development, skin, hair, body odour etc.
   - Sickle cell disease, where a mutation producing an abnormal haemoglobin has multiple serious phenotypic effects on all organ systems.

Using Chi-Squared in Genetics (page 154)

1. (a) H_0: "If both parents are heterozygous and there is independent assortment of alleles (no linkage) then we would expect to see a 9:3:3:1 ratio of phenotypes in the offspring ".
   (b) H_A: "If both parents are heterozygous and the genes are linked (i.e. on the same chromosome), then we would expect the ratios of phenotypes in the offspring to deviate from the 9:3:3:1".
2. (a) Completed table:

Category	O	E	O – E	$(O-E)^2$	$\frac{(O-E)^2}{E}$
Purple stem, jagged leaf	12	16.3	–4.3	18.5	1.1
Purple stem, smooth leaf	9	5.4	3.6	13	2.4
Green stem, jagged leaf	8	5.4	2.6	6.8	1.3
Green stem, smooth leaf	0	1.8	–1.8	3.2	1.8
	Σ 29				Σ 6.6

   Expected frequencies calculated as follows:
   Purple stem, jagged leaf = 9/16 x 29 = 16.3
   Purple stem, smooth leaf = 3/16 x 29 = 5.4
   Green stem, jagged leaf = 3/16 x 29 = 5.4
   Green stem, smooth leaf = 1/16 x 29 = 1.8
   Note: Whole numbers could be used in preference to rounding to one decimal place.
   (b) $\chi^2 = 6.6$
   (c) Degrees of freedom = (4-1=) 3
   (d) The critical value of χ^2 at $P = 0.05$ and at d.f.= 3 is 7.82. The calculated χ^2 value is less than the critical value (6.6 < 7.82).
   (e) We cannot reject H_0: There was no significant difference between the observed results and the expected phenotype ratio of 9:3:3:1. We must conclude that the genes controlling stem colour and leaf shape in tomatoes are on separate chromosomes (unlinked).
3. (a) H_0 and H_A as for question 1.
   (b) Completed table:

Category	O	E	O – E	$(O-E)^2$	$\frac{(O-E)^2}{E}$
Round-yellow seed	441	450	–9	81	0.18
Round-green seed	159	150	9	81	0.54
Wrinkled-yellow seed	143	150	–7	49	0.33
Wrinkled-green seed	57	50	7	49	0.98
	Σ 800				Σ 2.03

   Expected frequencies were calculated as follows:
   Round-yellow seed = 9/16 x 800 = 450
   Round-green seed = 3/16 x 800 = 150
   Wrinkled-yellow seed = 3/16 x 800 = 150
   Wrinkled-green seed = 1/16 x 800 = 50
   $\chi^2 = 2.03$
   (c) Degrees of freedom = (4-1) 3. The critical value of χ^2 at $P = 0.05$ and at d.f.= 3 is 7.82. The calculated χ^2 is less than the critical value (2.03 < 7.82).
   (d) We cannot reject H_0: There was no significant difference between the observed results and the expected phenotype ratio of 9:3:3:1. We must conclude that the genes controlling seed shape and colour are on separate chromosomes (unlinked).
4. In both cases, we cannot reject H_0, but in the first case, the χ^2 value is much higher. In the case of the tomatoes, the genes for stem colour and leaf shape **are** on separate chromosomes, but given the relatively large χ^2 value, repeating the experiment using more plants, or replicate setups, would serve as a check.

Gene-Environment Interactions (page 155)

1. Answer will vary based upon student's own choice, but examples include:
   Environment: The environment can alter the phenotype by altering the basic expression of a trait. Examples include: trees that are grown at high altitude are stunted in growth, trees exposed to a strong prevailing wind appear distorted in shape (windswept), poor nutrition in infancy can retard brain and bone development.
   Genotype: An organisms genotype has a major influence upon phenotype. Dominant alleles, recessive alleles, gene mutations, gene interactions, and epigenetics all influence phenotype. Examples include: albinism resulting from the inheritance of a recessive allele, the shape of the comb on a chicken depends on which allele combination they inherit, the colour of many flowers is determined by the dominance of one allele over another, and the colour of skin in humans is the result of six allele combinations.
2. Wind speed, temperature, air density, water availability.
3. In hydrangeas, the pH of the soil alters the colour of the flowers. In alkaline soils they are pink or red-purple, in acid soil the flowers are blue. The colour is due to the presence or absence of aluminium compounds in the flowers, and aluminium in the soil is only accessible to plants when soil pH is low. When aluminium is present within the plant, the flowers are blue. When

the aluminium is absent, the flowers are pink. **Note**: Growers may apply aluminium sulfate (sulphate) to the soil to lower the pH and produce blue flowers. Adding lime produces pink flowers.

4. These are the cooler parts of the body. Body heat is lost from these areas which make it cool enough for the enzyme responsible for colour-pointing to remain active.

5. To ensure genetic potential is reached, provide the optimum growth conditions for that plant. E.g. suitable water availability (water regularly), adequate nutrient supply (fertiliser application), sufficient sunlight (keep out of shade), equable temperature (warmth, protect from frost and wind), protection from pests and diseases (companion plant or spray for pests).

6. (a) A **cline** is a continuous, or nearly continuous, gradation in a phenotypic character within a species, associated with a change in an environmental variable such as temperature or wind.
   (b) **Plant A**: The observed phenotype (prostrate) of this species is not due to genetic factors, but to the effect of climate on growth patterns. In the absence of a harsh environment, the plant reverts to its normal growing habit.
   Plant B: The low growing phenotype of this species is controlled by genes (not environmental factors). Species B continued to be low growing.
   (c) Plant A is most likely to show clinal variation.

Small Flies and Giant Butterflies (page 160)

1. When the original species of drosophilidae arrived on the Hawaiian islands it found many new unoccupied niches into which it expanded, leading to an **adaptive radiation**.

2. The fruit flies are of interest because there are so many closely related species within a small area an speciation has been (and is) relatively frequent. The flies also have a relatively simple genome, making genetic studies relatively easy.

3. In general the oldest species of flies are found on the oldest islands. As islands appeared out of the sea the flies spread to new environments and diversified, giving rise to newer species.

4. Buttercups living in alpine areas periodically have their habitats reduced and their range restricted during periods of climatic warming. This restricts gene flow and leads to speciation.Periods of cooling allow for the expansion of their range and movement to new environments as well as hybridisation to form new species. Repeated many times, these cycles lead to a large range of species.

Gene Pools and Evolution (page 161)

1. & 2. **Note**: Do not include the beetle about to enter Deme 1 (aa) but do include the beetle about to leave Deme 1 (Aa). For the purpose of this exercise, assume that the individual with the mutation **A'A** in Deme 1 is a normal **AA** combination.

Deme 1: 22 beetles   Deme 2: 19 beetles

Deme 1		Number counted	%
Allele types	*A*	26	59.1
	a	18	40.9
Allele combinations	*AA*	8	36.4
	Aa	10	45.4
	aa	4	18.2

Deme 2		Number counted	%
Allele types	*A*	13	34.2
	a	25	65.8
Allele combinations	*AA*	1	5.3
	Aa	11	57.9
	aa	7	36.8

3. (a) **Population size**: Large population acts as a 'buffer' for random, directional changes in allele frequencies. A small population can exhibit changes in allele frequencies because of random loss of alleles (failure of an individual to contribute young to the next generation).
   (b) **Mate selection**: Random mating occurs in many animals and most plants. With 'mate selection', there is no random meeting of gametes, and certain combinations come together at a higher frequency than would occur by chance alone. This will alter the frequency of alleles in subsequent generations.
   (c) **Gene flow between populations**: Immigration (incoming) and emigration (outgoing) has the effect of adding or taking away alleles from a population that can change allele frequencies. In some cases, two-way movements may cancel, with no net effect.
   (d) **Mutations**: A source of new alleles. Most mutations are harmful, confer poor fitness, and will be lost from the gene pool over a few generations. Some may be neutral, conferring no advantage over organisms with different alleles. Occasionally, mutations may confer improved fitness and will increase in frequency with each generation, at the expense of other alleles.
   (e) **Natural selection**: Selection pressures will affect some allele types more than others, causing allele frequencies to change with each generation.

4. (a) Increase genetic variation: Gene flow (migration), large population size, mutation.
   (b) Decrease genetic variation: Natural selection, non-random mating (mate selection), genetic drift.

Hardy-Weinberg Calculations (page 163)

The answers to the panels provided in the workbook are shown below as working. Alternatively, these calculations are quickly done using a spreadsheet.

1. **Working**: q= 0.1, p= 0.9, q^2 = 0.01, p^2 = 0.81, 2pq=0.18
   Proportion of black offspring = 2pq + p^2 x 100% = 99%;
   Proportion of grey offspring = q^2 x 100% = 1%
2. **Working**: q= 0.3, p= 0.7, q^2 = 0.09, p^2 = 0.49, 2pq=0.42
   (a) Frequency of tall (dominant) gene (allele): 70%
   (b) 42% heterozygous; 42% of 400 = **168**
3. **Working**: q= 0.6, p= 0.4, q^2 = 0.36, p^2 = 0.16, 2pq=0.48
   (a) 40% dominant allele
   (b) 48% heterozygous; 48% of 1000 = **480**
4. **Working**: q= 0.2, p= 0.8, q^2 = 0.04, p^2 = 0.64, 2pq=0.32
   (a) 32% heterozygous (carriers)
   (b) 80% dominant allele
5. **Working**: q= 0.5, p= 0.5, q^2 = 0.25, p^2 = 0.25, 2pq= 0.5
   Proportion of population that becomes white = 25%
6. **Working**: q= 0.8, p= 0.2, q^2= 0.64, p^2= 0.04, 2pq= 0.32
   (a) 80% (c) 36% (e) 96%
   (b) 32% (d) 4%
7. **Working**: q= 0.1, p= 0.9, q^2= 0.01, p^2= 0.81, 2pq= 0.18
   Proportion of people expected to be albino (i.e. proportion that are homozygous recessive) = 1%

Analysis of a Squirrel Gene Pool (page 165)

1. Graph of population changes:

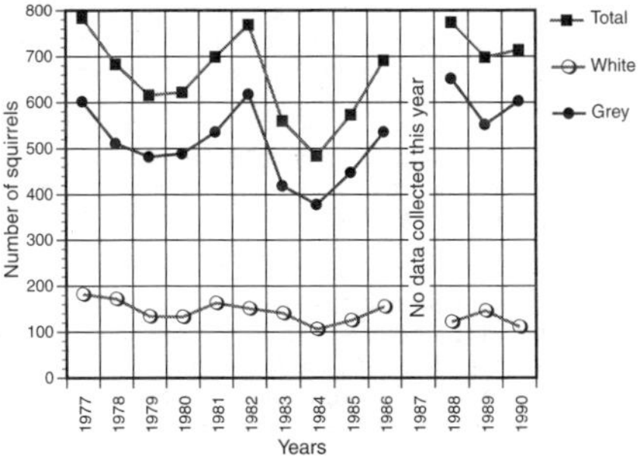

(a) 784 to 484 = 61% fluctuation
(b) Total population numbers exhibit an oscillation with a period of 5-6 years (2 cycles). Fluctuations occur in both normal grey and albino populations.

2. Graph of genotype changes:

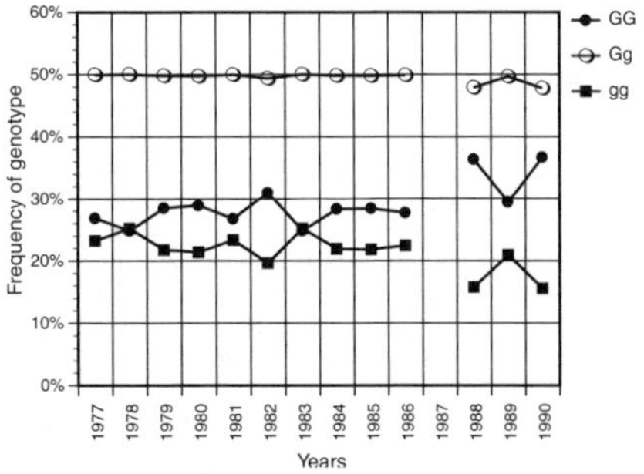

(a) GG genotype: Relatively constant frequency until the last 3-4 years which exhibit an increase. Could also argue that there is an increase over the total sampling period.
(b) Gg genotype: Uniform frequency.
(c) gg genotype: Relatively constant frequency until the last 3-4 years which exhibit a decline. Could also argue that there is a decrease over the total sampling period.

3. Graph of allele changes:

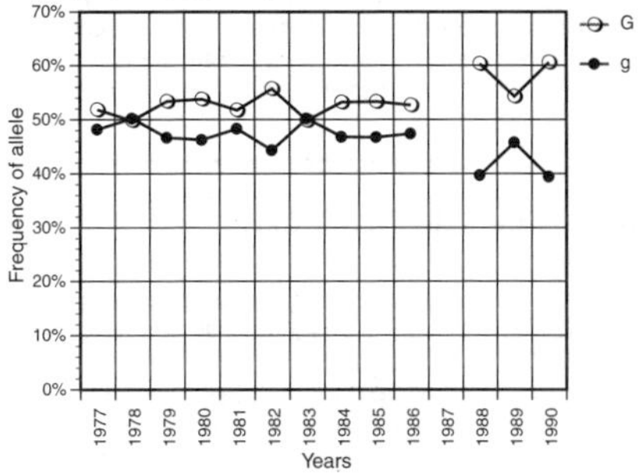

(a) Frequency of G: Increases in the last 3-4 years.
(b) Frequency of g: Decreases in the last 3-4 years.

4. (a) The frequency of alleles graph (to a lesser extent the frequency of genotypes graph)
   (b) Changes in allele frequencies in a population provide the best indication of significant evolutionary changes occurring. These cannot be deduced simply from changes in numbers or genotypes.
5. There are at least two possible causes (any one of):
   - Genetic drift in a relatively small population, i.e. there are random changes in allele frequencies as a result of small population size.
   - Natural selection against albinos. Albinism represents a selective disadvantage in terms of survival and reproduction (albinos are more vulnerable to predators because of greater visibility and have lower fitness generally).

Natural Selection (page 167)

1. Stable environments favour the most common phenotypes. Environmental instability provides a chance that extreme phenotypes might be advantageous, but in a stable environment, this is unlikely to happen. Predictability encourages a reduction in phenotypic variability because this is no disadvantage when the environment is largely static.

2. (a) Drought favoured birds with beak sizes at two extremes of the range, since these birds could exploit the small and the large seed sizes.
   (b) Continuation of the drought could lead to further divergence in beak size.
   (c) The selection pressures favouring a bimodal distribution in beak size would be reduced and medium sized beaks would become relatively more common (i.e. there would be a shift from disruptive to stabilising selection).

Black is the New Grey (page 168)

1. (a) The mutation for black coat colour shows incomplete dominance, so any mating involving a black squirrel will result in at least 50% dark coloured offspring (either brown black or jet black).
   (b) The black variant would spread more slowly through the population because two squirrels carrying the mutated gene for black coat colour would need to be mated together to produce dark coloured offspring.

Selection for Skin Colour in Humans (page 169)

1. (a) Folate is essential for healthy neural development. Note: A deficiency causes (usually fatal) neural tube defects (e.g. spina bifida).
   (b) Vitamin D is required for the absorption of dietary calcium and normal skeletal development. Note: A deficiency causes rickets in children or osteomalacia in adults. Osteomalacia in pregnancy can lead to pelvic fractures and inability to carry a pregnancy to term.

2. (a) Skin cancer normally develops after reproductive age and therefore protection against it provides no reproductive advantage and so no mechanism for selection.
   (b) The new hypothesis for the evolution of skin colour links the skin colour-UV correlation directly to evolutionary fitness (reproductive success). Skin needs to be dark enough to protect folate stores from destruction by UV and so prevent fatal neural defects in the offspring. However it also needs to be light enough to allow enough UV to penetrate the skin on order to manufacture vitamin D for calcium absorption. Without this, the female skeleton cannot successfully support a pregnancy. Because these pressures act on individuals both before and during reproductive age they provide a mechanism for selection. The balance of opposing selective pressures determines eventual skin colouration.

3. Women have a higher requirement for calcium during pregnancy and lactation. Calcium absorption is dependent on vitamin D, making selection pressure on females for lighter skins greater than for males.

4. The Inuit people have such abundant vitamin D in their diet that the selection pressure for lighter skin (for UV absorption and vitamin D synthesis) is reduced and their skin can be darker.

5. (a) Higher chances of getting rickets or (the adult equivalent) osteomalacia due to low UV absorption.
   (b) The simplest option to avoid these problems is for these people to take dietary supplements to increase the amount of vitamin D they obtain.

Industrial Melanism (page 171)

1. The appearance of the wings and body (how speckled and how dark the pigmentation).

2. (a) Selective agent is selective predation by birds.
   (b) The selection pressure (the differential effect of selective predation on survival) changed from favouring the survival of light coloured morphs in the unpolluted environments prior to the Industrial Revolution, to favouring the dark morph (over the light morph) during the Industrial Revolution (when there was a lot of soot pollution). In more recent times, with air quality improving, the survival of the light coloured morphs has once again improved.

3. There was a high frequency of the melanic form in and around industrial regions; the grey mottled form was more prevalent in non-industrial regions.

4. (a) Summer smoke from 75 to 15 $\mu g m^{-3}$ (80% drop). Winter SO_2 from 140 to 15 $\mu g m^{-3}$ (90% drop).
   (b) Melanic form frequency dropped from 95% to 50%.

5. In specific regions, the selection was directional, although over all of England, it could be considered disruptive (more correctly balancing), because different phenotypic extremes are favoured in different regions.

6. **Natural** selection occurs without human intervention, in response to normal environmental changes. In contrast, **artificial** selection is directed specifically by humans, usually towards a specific phenotypic result.

7. The environment (including the biotic environment) determines the selection pressures to which an organism will be exposed. It is these selection pressures that determine the fitness (differential survival and reproduction) or otherwise of an organism (with its particular set of allele combinations).

Heterozygous Advantage (page 173)

1. People who are heterozygous for the sickle cell gene are somewhat affected by sickle cell anaemia but have considerable resistance to malaria which is widespread in the region. This **heterozygous advantage** maintains the mutant allele at a relatively stable frequency in the population despite its deleterious effects. The stable coexistence of both the sickle cell allele and the normal allele exemplifies a **balanced polymorphism**.

Genetic Drift (page 174)

1. Genetic drift describes the random changes in allele frequencies in populations due to factors other than natural selection. Not all individuals, for various reasons, contribute their genes to the next generation.

The phenomenon is more pronounced in smaller populations that in larger ones.

2. Genetic drift reduces the amount of genetic variation in very small populations. Alleles may become eliminated altogether (0%) or become fixed (100%) as the only allele present in the gene pool for a particular gene.

3. Any endangered species with small numbers of individuals remaining: e.g. Puffin, monk seal, European lynx, otter, European beaver, hawksbill turtle, oryx, Siberian tiger (pop. ~500), Chinese tiger (pop. ~250), Sumatran tiger (pop. ~500), humpback whale, grey whale, blue whale.

The Founder Effect (page 175)

1.

Mainland	Nos	%		Nos	%
Allele A	48	54.5	Black	11	25
Allele a	40	45.5	Dark	26	59
Total	88	100	Pale	7	16
Island	**Nos**	**%**		**Nos**	**%**
Allele A	12	75	Black	4	50
Allele a	4	25	Dark	4	50
Total	16	100	Pale	0	0

2. The frequency of the dominant allele (A) is higher on the island population.

3. (a) Plants: Seeds are carried by wind, birds and water.
   (b) Animals: Reach islands largely by 'rafting', whereby animals are carried offshore while clinging to vegetation; some animals survive better than others.
   (c) Non-marine birds: Blown off course and out to sea by a storm. Birds with strong stamina may survive.

4. Genetic drift: Small populations may suffer random, non-directional changes in the frequency of an allele.

Population Bottlenecks (page 176)

1. A sudden decrease in the size of a population can result in a corresponding reduction in genetic variation. This means the population has limited 'genetic resources' to cope with the selection pressures imposed on it. In particular, it is seen as reduced reproductive success and greater sensitivity to disease.

2. Poor genetic diversity means that if one individual is susceptible to a disease, then they are all likely to be vulnerable; a direct result of reduced genetic diversity.

3. With reduced genetic diversity, selection pressures acting on the population are likely to have devastating effects on survival if one trait is found to be unsuited. Since all cheetahs are virtually identical in their traits, if one individual is vulnerable to a selection pressure, then they will all succumb.

The Biological Species Concept (page 177)

1. Behavioural (they show no interest in each other).

2. Physical barrier; sea separating Australia from SE Asia.

3. The red wolf is rare and may have difficulty finding another member of its species to mate with.

4. The populations on the two land masses, which have identical appearance and habitat requirements, were connected relatively recently by a land bridge during the last ice age (about 18 000 years ago). This would have permitted breeding between the populations. Individuals from the current populations have been brought together and are able to interbreed and produce fertile offspring.

5. The biological species concept cannot be applied to all situations nor to all organisms. It can rarely be applied to extinct organisms, nor to organisms that reproduce asexually. Asexual organisms include bacteria, but also parthenogenetic eukaryotes, and many plants which hybridise easily and reproduce solely by vegetative means. Organsims (including many birds) also interbreed freely to produce fertile hybrids, making their species boundaries unclear.

Isolating Mechanisms (page 178)

1. Isolating mechanisms protect the gene pool from the diluting and potentially adverse effects of introduced genes. Species are finely tuned to their niche; foreign genes will usually reduce fitness.

2. (a) Geographical isolation physically separates populations (and gene pools) but, if reintroduced, the two populations could potentially interbreed, i.e. reproductive isolation may not have occurred.
   (b) Geographical isolation enables populations to diverge in response to different selection pressures and (potentially) develop reproductive isolating mechanisms. Reproductive isolation won't generally occur in a populations in which there is gene flow (unless by special events such as polyploidy).

3. Geographical isolation physically separates populations (gene pools) so there is no gene flow between them. Ecological isolation arises as a result of different preferences in habitat or behaviour even though the populations occupy the same geographical area.

Reproductive Isolation (page 179)

1. (a) Postzygotic: hybrid breakdown
   (b) Prezygotic: structural
   (c) Prezygotic: temporal
   (d) Postzygotic: hybrid inviability

2. They are a secondary backup if the first isolating mechanism fails. The majority of species do not interbreed because of prezygotic mechanisms. Postzygotic mechanisms are generally rarer events.

The Phylogenetic Species Concept (page 181)

1. (a) Under the PSC, species are assigned on the basis of shared derived characteristics, which may be morphological or biochemical. A species is the smallest group that all share a derived character state.
   (b) Problems (one of):
   It can lead to a proliferation of species that are difficult to distinguish.
   It is difficult to justify its application to morphological distinct but interbreeding populations.
   (c) The PSC might be more appropriate than the BSC for extinct organisms, and for asexually reproducing

organisms such as bacteria.

2. Genetic techniques can be used to trace the occurrence of new character states and distinguish species on the basis of a unique combination of characters. Taxa that share more derived characters are more closely related than those that share fewer. This produces a hierarchy of shared character states, which leads to a tree of relatedness.

Breeding Modern Wheat (page 182)

1. Any three of the following:
   Large grain size, high gluten (protein) content, high yield, less tendency for stalks to break, disease resistance, non-shattering heads.

2. The evolution of modern wheat involved two natural hybridisation events accompanied by polyploidy to restore fertility. These events produced emmar and common wheat, which were selected under cultivation for increased yield, pest and disease resistance, and high protein content. Recent selection techniques have enabled these desirable traits to be tagged to markers, which increases the efficiency of the selection process and ensures the selection process (the gain towards the desirable phenotype) proceeds more rapidly.

Designer Herds (page 183)

1. Artificial selection can achieve genetic gains (gain toward the desired phenotype) much more rapidly because mating is carefully controlled and only a few phenotypes are permitted to breed. This accelerates the loss of unwanted alleles from the gene pool.

2. Gain from selective breeding has been rapid in cattle because of the intense selection of superior bulls and the widespread (national and international) use of their semen to produce a large number of progeny through AI. Herds are carefully managed and matings and progeny are documented, so the bulls and cows with the best genetics are selected to breed.

Darwin: Pigeon Fancier? (page 184)

1. Darwin was worried he would be ridiculed if he had no "experimental" evidence to support his theory that species could change over time. He saw the rapid changes achievable in pigeon breeds as good evidence for what could be achieved when a selection process was applied to populations.

2. A huge variety in pigeon morphology was generated by selective breeding from a generalised ancestor (the rock pigeon). These changes were not superficial, but extended to features of the skeleton too. Darwin suggested that, if such dramatic changes were achievable in a short time by a directed process, surely similarly large changes in morphology could occur over millions of years in natural populations subjected to different environments.

What is Cloning? (page 186)

1. Reproductive cloning is used to create an organism that is identical to another, already existing, organism. It involves transfer of an egg containing transplanted genetic material to the uterus of a surrogate, where development proceeds normally. In contrast, non-reproductive cloning aims only to produce embryos for the purpose of harvesting of embryonic stem cells. The clones for this purpose may be produced using nuclear transfer (as in reproductive cloning) or (more commonly) they may be IVF embryos donated for research. They are not permitted to develop past the blastocyst stage at which point they are (usually) sacrificed for the harvest of stem cells.

2. If advances in technology permit embryos to survive after ESC have been removed, then one of the major ethical barriers to the harvest of ESC (death of an embryo) is also removed. If this is the case, the technology becomes more ethically acceptable to more people and should proceed more rapidly.

3. A reproductively cloned organism may not be genetically identical to its donor because of the effects of random mutation and because of genetic material acquired from the mitochondrial DNA (in the egg to which the nuclear DNA was transferred).

Vegetative Propagation (page 187)

1. **Vegetative propagation** refers to the asexual means by which plants reproduce themselves. Natural means include rhizomes, tubers and runners. Artificial means include grafting and cuttings.

2. Enables the plant to have an overwintering food store from which it can mobilise food early on in the next growing season. This gives the plant a head start on plants that rely only on photosynthesis (light levels are often low early in the growing season).

3. Vegetative propagation has enabled the production of large numbers of plants from one successful (e.g. high yielding) variety. Successful combinations of genetic characteristics can be retained through vegetative propagation.

4. Vegetative reproduction enables a well adapted plant to spread rapidly and saturate its environment, out-competing plants that must wait to produce seeds.

5. (a) Vegetative propagation is a useful conservation strategy because it enables large numbers of plants to be produced without having to wait for them to set seed and reproduce sexually.
   (b) If plants are rare, vegetative propagation can boost numbers so that they are in a more viable population position. When less at risk, sexual propagation (pollination and fertilisation) methods can be included.
   (c) Species reliant on vegetative propagation may lack the genetic diversity to remain viable. Genetic diversity is an important part of being able to produce adaptive phenotypes in cases of environmental change.

6. A **cutting** is a portion of the parent plant that is removed and induced to grow into a new individual. Cuttings are used when one wants to merely propagate the features of the plant from which the cutting was

taken. **Grafting** is a more complicated procedure where a scion from one individual is joined to the shoot of another plant (the rootstock). Grafting is used to incorporate the (favourable) features of two individual plants and produce a superior variety.

Plant Tissue Culture (page 189)

1. The purpose of tissue culture is to produce large numbers of clones (with identical phenotypic and genetic traits as the parent) in a short space of time.
2. (a) A **callus** is a mass of undifferentiated cells.
   (b) Several plant hormones are added to the culture in sequence to stimulate each phase of development.
3. Compared with traditional propagation methods, tissue culture has a number of advantages. Tissue culture enables the production of many clones from a single seed/explant and allows the selection of desirable traits directly from culture. It facilitates rapid propagation, with no wait for seed production and is ideal for plants with long generation times, low seed production, or seeds that are difficult to germinate. Tissue culture also facilitates the international exchange of plants without quarantine and allows researchers to eliminate plant diseases from propagation lines. It is also space saving and overcomes seasonal restrictions to propagation. However, there are several disadvantages to this technology. Tissue culture is very labour intensive and trial and error is necessary to determine the ideal culturing conditions. Cultured plants may be genetically unstable/infertile and, over time, there may be a loss of genetic diversity (see Q4.).
4. Continued culture of a limited number of cloned varieties leads to a change in the genetic composition of the population (the amount of genetic variation decreases). This reduces the amount of variation upon which the gene pool can draw in times of change. This in turn reduces the ability (of the gene pool) to adapt.

Cloning by Nuclear Transfer (page 191)

1. The birth of Dolly showed that a clone could be produced using non-embryonic (somatic) tissue of a known phenotype. Dolly as the first mammal to be cloned using non-embryonic cells in this way.
2. (a) **Switching off genes in the donor cell**: Induced by low nutrient medium (starvation of the egg).
   (b) **Fusion of donor and enucleated egg**: Induced by a short electric pulse.
   (c) **Activation of the cloned cell (reconstructed egg cell)**: Induced by a second gentle electric pulse or by chemical means. A time delay of about 6 hours improves the success of the egg activation process, probably through the prolonged contact of the chromatin with (unknown) cytoplasmic factors.
3. Potential applications (a) and (b) any two of:
   - Production of clones from a proven phenotype that can quickly be disseminated to commercial herds.
   - Rapid production of transgenic animals that produce a particular product (e.g. a pharmaceutical secreted in milk), in order to respond to a market demand.
   - Conservation of rare livestock breeds. It is hoped that cloning will eventually be integrated into zoo management programmes. By retaining the tissues of individuals before they die, some of the genetic diversity of rare species can be retained. It may even be possible to restore species that are on the verge of extinction using cloning technology.

Cloning by Embryo Splitting (page 193)

1. (a) **Embryo splitting** is a much simpler technique than nuclear transfer and involves only the splitting of a normally produced embryo at a very early stage in development. The embryos continue to develop normally (as in the case of natural identical twins). There is no inducement of a somatic cell.
   (b) One disadvantage of embryo splitting is that the clones are derived from an embryo whose physical characteristics are not completely known. This makes the process more lengthy than with SCNT which involves cloning cells from an adult of known phenotype.
2. Cloned early stage embryos are a potential source of embryonic stem cells (ESC). These undifferentiated cells can (potentially) be induced to develop into any type of tissue in the recipient (a similar outcome for the production of blood cells is already achieved with bone marrow transplants).
3. Unless carefully managed, continued use of cloning technologies could potentially reduce the total pool of genetic diversity from which to select new breeds/strains/varieties.

KEY TERMS: Word Find (page 194)

L	L	C	T	H	E	R	A	P	E	U	T	I	C	C	L	O	N	I	N	G	I	T	N	A
R	D	S	Z	A	Y	B	R	O	O	T	S	T	O	C	K	U	C	H	Z	R	K	W	V	C
I	D	E	M	B	R	Y	O	S	P	L	I	T	T	I	N	G	L	T	Q	Q	C	I	H	H
P	U	Q	R	E	P	R	O	D	U	C	T	I	V	E	C	L	O	N	I	N	G	A	D	E
C	S	C	N	T	X	J	T	F	B	L	A	S	T	O	C	Y	S	T	K	E	K	V	B	M
W	Y	W	C	U	T	T	I	N	G	I	J	F	N	D	J	V	E	N	Z	M	S	L	E	C
O	U	D	A	R	O	I	F	M	P	S	P	Z	X	S	U	C	K	E	R	B	V	T	I	P
R	M	I	C	R	O	P	R	O	P	A	G	A	T	I	O	N	H	A	H	R	P	A	U	N
P	R	I	C	Y	G	F	F	K	T	Z	Y	B	M	Q	X	W	L	O	Y	Y	K	U	X	U
G	X	K	T	I	S	S	U	E	C	U	L	T	U	R	E	I	O	I	K	O	Y	X	U	U
P	P	E	D	C	E	E	Z	Q	G	D	Y	I	S	R	O	F	K	L	Z	N	I	X	Q	P
X	M	M	F	B	L	C	O	M	O	S	K	W	W	B	A	G	X	C	X	I	X	Y	D	O
F	H	U	J	E	Z	W	T	U	U	W	H	H	C	L	O	N	E	T	M	C	O	U	Z	Z
V	W	H	U	Y	N	K	S	L	D	W	B	J	Z	C	S	T	E	M	C	E	L	L	S	J
W	P	C	Y	C	W	Y	P	E	C	Y	H	E	I	T	O	H	G	R	A	F	T	I	N	G
Z	M	J	J	B	F	T	F	L	R	H	I	Z	O	M	E	R	U	T	U	B	E	R	R	H
M	W	R	K	G	O	T	H	U	P	B	M	H	B	Q	O	W	M	H	K	U	S	N	X	L

Microbes and Biotechnology (page 197)

1. A continuous culture system provides a constant supply of fresh culture medium while removing product/spend culture at the same rate. In contrast, a batch culture adds cells to a fixed volume of medium and the process is halted when the appropriate stage of culture growth has been reached.
2. This keeps the cells actively growing and dividing (this is when they produce the product). It is undesirable for them to enter the stationary phase (which they would do if they exhausted the growth medium).
3. Batch culture is used when a secondary metabolite is being harvested.
4. Asepsis prevents the contamination of the culture with

undesirable organisms which, if present, may compete with the desirable microbes and cause a change in the nature or quality of the end product, low product yield, and loss of time and profit.

5. (a) Heat can be dissipated by using a water jacket (containing cool water). It is assisted by the physical mixing of the culture.
   (b) Oxygen demand is met by aerating the culture using a diffuser (sparger), a perforated disc which disperses air through the medium.
   (c) Nutrient levels are monitored throughout the culture process and demand is met by addition of new culture medium (or end-harvest) when indicated.

Microbial Growth and Metabolites (page 199)

1. (a) The initial lag is a result of the fact that there is little or no cell division occurring, hence no perceivable growth in cell number (the cells are increasing in size and synthesising enzymes, but not dividing).
   (b) The lag can be reduced by placing actively dividing cells into a new culture medium (i.e. starting with actively dividing cells).

2. Adding fresh nutrients and removing toxic by-products keeps the culture in the maximal log phase of growth. This is especially important if the product being harvested is a primary metabolite.

3. (a) Because it is produced as a product of metabolism.
   (b) Secondary metabolites are not immediately essential for microbial survival but are produced at the end of the active growth phase, so the maximum yield occurs after growth slows.

4. Primary metabolite is a product that is formed at the same time as the cells (growth and production curves are similar). Secondary metabolites are produced after the microbe has largely completed it growth and has entered the stationary phase.

5. Secondary metabolites are produced in response to depletion of nutrients or build-up of waste products, often as a defence or competitive strategy. They therefore are not produced until active growth has slowed.

Soy Sauce Production (page 201)

1. Crushing breaks up the grains/beans. This makes the starch more accessible as a substrate for the fungus.

2. (a) *Aspergillus* breaks down the proteins in the wheat-soy mash to release amino acids and peptides.
   (b) Lactic acid bacteria (by lactic acid fermentation) metabolise the carbohydrates in the koji to produce lactic acid. They also metabolise peptides to produce amino acids.
   (c) Yeasts (by alcoholic fermentation) metabolise carbohydrates in the koji to produce alcohol. They also metabolise peptides to produce amino acids.

3. (a) Soy produced using chemical hydrolysis lacks the flavour profile and natural colour contributed by the products of fermentation. It also has alcohols and esters, which contribute an inferior aroma and a different feel in the mouth.
   (b) It is much quicker (and therefore less expensive) than a fermentation (a few days as opposed to several months or more).

Environmental Biotechnology (page 202)

1. (a) and (b) any of:
   - Bacterial oxidation of organic matter in sewage.
   - GM bacteria used for detecting specific pollutants.
   - Use of bacteria to metabolise hydrocarbons in oil.

2. Compared with traditional mining techniques, biomining is simpler, therefore more cost-effective, less damaging to the environment, and uses biological processes to recover metals from low grade ores that would otherwise be unprofitable to mine.

Industrial Production of Enzymes (page 203)

1. Benefits of microbial enzymes in industry include:
   - Huge microbial diversity: this is important because a wide variety of microbial enzymes are available.
   - Microbial culture is relatively straightforward, so the enzymes are cost effective to produce for industry.
   - The enzymes can be immobilised and so used repeatedly and recovered (thus reducing costs).
   - The enzymes often do not require highly specific conditions in which to operate, so industrial processes can proceed at standard temperatures and pressures. Specific enzymes are also available to catalyse reactions where specific conditions (e.g. high temperatures) are required.

2. (a) In the production of **intracellular enzymes**, the microbial cells must first be separated from the culture medium and then disrupted. The production of **extracellular enzymes** does not require this cellular disruption.
   (b) Cellular disruption is required to release intracellular enzymes from within the cells. Extracellular enzymes are present in the medium after being secreted by the cells.

3. A crude extract is cheaper to produce in cases where a highly purified product is not required.

Putting Enzymes to Use (page 204)

1. (a) Cell free enzyme extracts generally show a high level of activity. This makes them an efficient option for industrial processes, especially those with a limited number of steps.
   (b) A cell free extract might not be used if (any of):
   - The processes involved in production of the end product were complex (involving several intracellular enzymes).
   - The enzyme involved was unstable or inactive outside the cell.

2. (a) Benefits of immobilised enzymes. Any two of:
   - Easy recovery of enzyme for reuse.
   - Easy harvesting of enzyme-free end-product.
   - Greater stability (protection of a solid matrix).
   - Continuous fermentation is possible
   - Keeps proteolytic enzymes apart so that they do not digest each other.
   - Lower cost (because enzymes can be reused).
   (b) Disadvantage of immobilised enzymes. Any of:
   - Immobilisation may be difficult to achieve.

- Immobilisation may lower enzyme activity and reaction rates.
- Immobilisation technique may not be stable; enzymes may eventually wash away.

(c) Factors affecting the rate of end-product harvest (any of): Supply of substrate, temperature, pH, method of immobilisation (if any).

3. Enzymes are proteins, therefore proteases could break each other down. Immobilisation holds proteolytic enzyme molecules apart from each other on an inert material so that they do not interact. In this way, the active life of the enzymes is prolonged.

4. Any of the following reasons
   - Encapsulation may make it difficult for enzyme and substrate to interact.
   - Covalent bonding may damage the enzyme or subtly interfere with the active site.
   - Entrapment may affect charges on the enzyme and affect interaction with the substrate. The enzyme may also leak away.
   - Reaction rates may be slowed if rates of diffusion of substrate and end-product into and out of a matrix are reduced.
   - Adsorbed enzymes are not firmly attached and may wash away.

Applications of Enzymes (page 205)

1. (a) The reaction would not proceed or would require high temperatures or pressures to make it proceed.
   (b) The reaction would proceed only slowly.
   Both consequences add expense to a process.

2. Properties of microbial enzymes that make them suitable industrial catalysts. (a)-(c) any three of:
   - Huge microbial diversity: important because it means that there is a wide variety of microbial enzymes available.
   - Microbial culture is relatively straightforward, so the enzymes are cost effective to produce for industry.
   - The enzymes can be immobilised and so used repeatedly and recovered (thus reducing costs).
   - The enzymes often do not require highly specific conditions in which to operate, so industrial processes can proceed at standard temperatures and pressures. Specific enzymes are also available to catalyse reactions where specific conditions (e.g. high temperatures) are required.

3. Correction: Question should read "Choose one example from those described in the diagram **on the previous page**...." Brief answers only (one example given; there are often others). Students might provide more detail.

   (a) **Chymosin** from GE yeast or bacteria (including *E. coli* (Chy-max in the US) and *Kluyveromyces lactis*).
   (b) Used to coagulate the milk protein, casein.

   (a) **Amyloglucosidases** from GE bacteria.
   (b) Used to speed up the conversion of starch to sugars to get a low-calorie beer. **Note**: **proteases**, from GE microbes are used to modify the proteins from the malt and prevent cloudiness in the finishing stage. These are in addition to the proteases arising naturally from the grain in germination, which solubilise the proteins in the grains and make the amino acids available to the yeast.

   (a) **Pectinases** from the soft-rot bacterium *Erwinnia* or from GE *Aspergillus niger*.
   (b) Breaks down the soluble pectin chains remaining in pressed juice and reduces cloudiness.

   (a) **Citrate synthase** is produced by a mutant strain of the fungus *Aspergillus niger*.
   (b) Citrate synthase (also isocitrate dehydrogenase), catalyses the fermentation of sucrose (under nitrogen limitation) to citric acid, a widely used preservative and pH regulator in the food industry.

   (a) **Proteases** from *Bacillus subtilis*.
   (b) Break the peptide bonds in protein-based stains.

   (a) **Invertase** (sucrase) from *Saccharomyces* spp.
   (b) Converts sucrose to glucose and fructose (invert syrup) to produce a soft centre in sweets.

   (a) **Glucose oxidase** from the fungus *Aspergillus niger*.
   (b) Used in medical biosensors for the detection of blood glucose level. Glucose oxidase catalyses the conversion of the glucose to gluconic acid.

   (a) **Proteases** from *Bacillus subtilis*.
   (b) Break the peptide bonds in proteins, and digesting the hair and tissue from animal hides.

   (a) **Lactase** from the bacterium *Kluyveromyces lactis*.
   (b) Converts lactose to glucose and galactose in low lactose dairy products.

   (a) **Ligninases** from white rot fungal species.
   (b) Breaks down the lignin in wood pulp and wood waste. Lignin is a complex molecule and several enzymes, including laccase, lignin peroxidase, and manganese peroxidase are involved.

4. (a) Biosensors use biological material, e.g. an enzyme, to detect the presence or concentration of a particular substance. **Note**: The biological material is immobilised within a semi-conductor. Its activity (in response to the substrate), causes an ion change which is detected by a transducer, amplified, and displayed as a read-out.
   (b) An enzyme that uses alcohol as its substrate (e.g. alcohol dehydrogenase) could be immobilised in the biological recognition layer. The product of its activity (on alcohol) would produce a detectable change, which would be amplified and displayed as a read-out.

5. (a) Microbial proteases are used in the pre-tanning processes of leather manufacture (e.g. removing fat and hair from hides). The ease with which they can be produced and the wide range of enzymes available has reduced the costs of leather treatment since they need not be pure formulations to be effective. Microbial proteases are also safer and more environmentally-friendly than the toxic chemicals traditionally used in tanning (tannery effluent has long been a source of environmental pollution from a range of chemicals including lime, sodium sulfide, salt, and organic solvents and dyes).
   (b) Chymosin from microbial sources has replaced much of the rennet from calves stomachs traditionally used in cheese production. Chymosin produced from GE microbial sources is very pure and therefore more predictable in terms of its activity than its traditional rennet counterpart. Microbial chymosin can also be produced quickly,

so fluctuating demands can be easily satisfied. Fewer calves are required when microbial sources of chymosin supplement the traditional sources and the cheese from made using microbial chymosin is acceptable to vegetarians and others who will not eat cheese made with calf rennet. These features have (respectively) improved the efficiency, cost effectiveness, and consumer appeal of the product made with microbial chymosin.

(c) The use of fungal ligninases to treat wood waste has improved the environmental safety and reduced pollution over the traditional methods (such as organic sulfur compounds). Fungal treatment of wood waste effectively accelerates natural biodegradation processes and allows these to continue even at cooler temperatures. Wood waste treated in this way is suitable for use as compost or in mushroom production.

What is Genetic Modification? (page 208)

1. Organisms may be genetically modified through:
   - The addition of a foreign gene, e.g. human insulin gene inserted into bacteria or yeast for the commercial production of human insulin.
   - Alteration of an existing gene so that a protein is expressed at a higher rate or in a different way. This GM technique is used in gene therapy.
   - Deletion or inactivation of an existing gene, e.g. the Flavr-Savr tomato which has had its ripening gene switched off. Gene inactivation also produces 'knock-out mice' which are used to study the physiological effects of particular genes.

2. (a) **Gene therapy**: A need/desire to find cures/ treatments for genetic diseases (e.g. cystic fibrosis).
   (b) **Transgenic organisms**: A need to accelerate traditional breeding programmes by direct manipulation of the genome and a desire to improve the usefulness of livestock and crops by increasing production and reducing susceptibility to diseases and pests. There has also been a desire (need?) to produce new protein products by providing novel genes to make plants and animals into biofactories.
   (c) **Plant micropropagation**: A desire for quick, large scale propagation of plant clones with superior traits, a need for disease free specimens, and a need to overcome seasonal growing restrictions.

Restriction Enzymes (page 209)

1. (a) **Restriction enzyme**: Enzymes that cut DNA at very precise base sequences (they are able to create sticky end or blunt end junctions). They can be used to remove pieces of DNA from one organism for insertion into a vector or another organism.
   (b) **Recognition site**: The base sequence that a restriction enzyme "recognises" and cuts.
   (c) **Sticky end**: The exposed ends of DNA after a restriction enzyme has cut, leaving a partially unmatched base sequence.
   (d) **Blunt end**: DNA cut leaving no sticky end. May be joined to any other blunt end fragment (not specific).

2. (a) *Eco*RI
   (b) *Escherichia coli* RY13
   (c) GAATTC

3. (a) GGATCC
   (b) Recognition sites: See the diagram below.
   (c) 5 DNA fragments

4. There is a need to have a tool kit of enzymes that allows scientists to cut DNA at any point they wish. The action of such enzymes allows DNA to be manipulated for other recombinant DNA technologies.

Ligation (page 210)

1. (a) **Annealing**: The two single-stranded DNA molecules are recombined into double-stranded form (achieved by H-bonding between complementary bases).
   (b) **DNA ligase**: This enzyme joins two adjacent pieces of DNA by linking nucleotides in the sticky ends.

2. DNA ligase performs the task of linking together the Okazaki fragments during DNA replication.

3. It joins together DNA molecules, while restriction enzymes cut them up.

Gel Electrophoresis (page 211)

1. Purpose of **gel electrophoresis**: To separate mixtures of molecules (proteins, nucleic acids) on the basis of size and other physical properties.

2. (a) The frictional (retarding) force of each fragment's size (larger fragments travel more slowly than smaller ones).
   (b) The strength of the electric field (movement is more rapid in a stronger field).
   Note: The temperature and the ionic strength of the buffer can be varied to optimise separation.

3. The gel is full of pores (holes) through which the fragments must pass. Smaller fragments pass through these pores more easily (with less resistance and therefore faster) than larger ones.

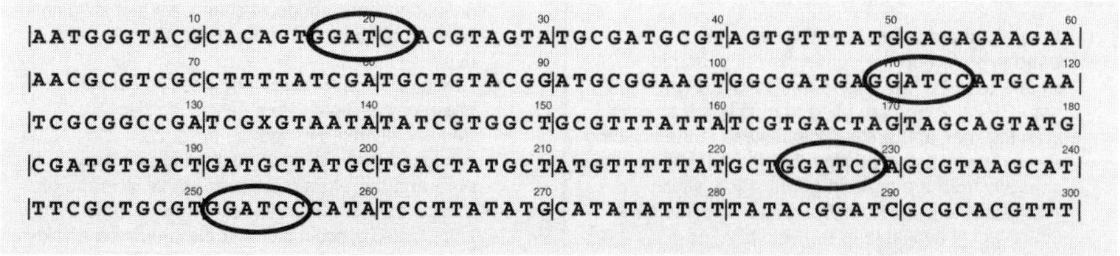

Polymerase Chain Reaction (page 213)

1. To produce large quantities of 'cloned' DNA from very small samples. Large quantities are needed for effective analysis. Very small quantities are often unusable.

2. A double stranded DNA is heated to 98°C for 5 min, causing the two strands to separate. Primers, free nucleotides, and DNA polymerase are added to the sample. The sample is then cooled to 60°C for a few minutes, and the primers anneal to the DNA strands. The sample is incubated and complementary strands are created (by the DNA polymerase) using each strand of the DNA sample as a template. (Incubation temperature depends on the particular polymerase used; it is ~72°C for heat tolerant *Taq* polymerase, but lower for other polymerases). The process is repeated about 25 times, each time the number of templates doubles over the previous cycle.

3. (a) Forensic samples taken at the scene of a crime (e.g. hair, blood, semen).
   (b) Archaeological samples from early human remains.
   (c) Samples taken from the remains of prehistoric organisms preserved in ice, mummified, preserved in amber, tar pits etc.

4. This exercise can be done on a calculator by pressing the 1 button (for the original sample) and then multiplying by 2 repeatedly (to simulate each cycle).
   (a) 1024
   (b) 33 554 432 (33.5 million)

5. (a) It would be amplified along with the intended DNA sample, thereby contaminating the sample and rendering it unusable.
   (b) Sources of contamination (any two of):
   Dirty equipment (equipment that has DNA molecules left on it from previous treatments).
   DNA from the technician (dandruff from the technician is a major source of contamination!)
   Spores, viruses and bacteria in the air.
   (c) Precautions to avoid contamination (any two of):
   Using disposable equipment (pipette tips, gloves).
   Wearing a **head cover** (disposable cap).
   Use of **sterile procedures**.
   Use of **plastic disposable tubes with caps** that seal the contents from air contamination.

6. (a) and (b) any of the following procedures require a certain minimum quantity of DNA in order to be useful: DNA sequencing, gene cloning, DNA profiling, transformation, making artificial genes. Descriptions of these procedures are provided in the workbook.

Manual DNA Sequencing (page 215)

1. (a) **Forensic science**: Samples of blood, semen, and hair left at the scene of a crime can be used to identify the perpetrator of a crime.
   (b) **Legal disputes**: Arguments over paternity of humans (and lately, the pedigree of racehorses).
   (c) **Medical applications**: Identification of genetic disorders in humans to provide opportunity for genetic counselling.
   (d) **Evolution/taxonomy**: Determining the genetic relatedness of groups of plants and animals to reassess the traditional classification models for those organisms (to produce a phylogenetic tree which reflects their evolutionary relationships).
   (e) **Archeology/anthropology**: Studies of the genetic makeup of modern human races to determine the geographic origin of modern humans and the timing of this event.
   (f) **Conservation of endangered species**: Studies of populations of threatened species to determine the degree of genetic biodiversity. This is important for endangered species that have small populations with low genetic diversity due to in-breeding. The degree to which populations are genetically isolated from each other can also be determined.
   (g) **Livestock breeding programs**: Assist with the tracking of offspring from matings between livestock parents. Will also assist in the identification of transgenic offspring from mated transgenic parents.

2. The Human Genome Project required an **automated process** that could cope with the sequencing of the 3 billion bases making up the human genome. It has to be automated, rapid, and cost-effective (cheap to run).

Genome Analysis (page 219)

1. (a) **Genome mapping**: Locates the exact position of all the genes on the various chromosomes. Produce genetic and physical maps of varying resolution.
   (b) **Genome sequencing**: Determines the precise nucleotide (base) sequence for each gene. From this can be determined the gene product (protein).

2. A **clone library** (also known as a gene library) is a collection of cloned DNA sequences representative of the entire genome of the organism under study. The cloned DNA sequences reside in the accessory chromosomes of other organisms (yeast, bacteria) into which they are placed (each type of fragment resides in a separate culture). In contrast, a **subclone library** is a collection of much smaller DNA fragments (1500-5000 bp), each inserted into a plasmid vector and cloned.

3. (a) **Restriction enzymes**: The genome is cut up using restriction enzymes in preparation for creating a clone library and subclone library.
   (b) **Ligation**: DNA fragments are inserted into vectors using DNA ligation to create a clone library and subclone library.
   (c) **PCR**: The positions of DNA markers on each fragment are determined using PCR (and gel electrophoresis).
   (d) **Gel electrophoresis**: The positions of DNA markers on a fragment are determined using gel electrophoresis (and PCR). Gel electrophoresis is also used to sequence each small DNA fragment to determine the exact base sequence.

4. DNA markers provide genetic landmarks along the length of DNA being sequenced. These are used to assemble the sequences for each of the fragments in the correct order.

Investigating Genetic Biodiversity (page 221)

1. A **proteinase** enzyme dissolves the tissues of the springtails to release the DNA from the cells.

2. (a) *Taq* polymerase binds to the DNA primers and synthesises the complementary strands of DNA.
   (b) Nucleotides are added to the PCR mixture because

the polymerase requires the free nucleotides to synthesise the complementary DNA strands.

(c) The high temperature (92°C) separates the strands of DNA. The lower temperature (45°C) causes the primers to anneal to each DNA strand. The sample is then incubated at 72°C because this is the optimum working temperature for the Taq polymerase (a thermophilic bacterial enzyme) which synthesises the complementary DNA strands.

3. (a) The **negative** will be any substance devoid of DNA, e.g. water or some chemical solution blank.
(b) The **reference** (=the ladder) provides a reference position for fragments of known length to which the sample fragments can be compared. The fragment length in the sample can then be determined.

4. (a) A point mutation (gene mutation involving a change to one nucleotide).
(b) The point mutation has occurred to the first base of a codon. Unlike mutations to the third base, which are less likely to change the amino acid coded for, a change to the first base will cause a change in the amino acid. Another amino acid will form part of the polypeptide chain made from this gene.

The Human Genome Project (page 223)

1. **HGP**: Aims to map the entire base sequence of every chromosome in the human cell (our genome), to identify all genes in the sequence, determine what they express (protein produced), and determine the precise role of every gene on the chromosomes.
HGDP: The HGDP aims to map the differences in genomes between different racial and ethnic groups.

2. Genomic differences on the basis of race could be misused for discriminatory purposes.

3. (a) **Medical** (any of the following):
- Will identify the location and sequence for up to 4000 known genetic diseases, opening up opportunities for drug therapy.
- Will provide the information to enable the production of human proteins to correct metabolic deficiencies.
- Will open up the possibility of gene therapy for many genetic diseases.
- Will enable the development of new therapeutic drugs to block metabolic pathways.
- With greater knowledge, emphasis will shift from treatment of disease to better diagnosis and prevention of disease.
- Screening for genetic predisposition to disease.
- The ability to sequence quickly and directly will revolutionise mutation research (direct study of the link between mutagens and their effects).

(b) **Non-medical** (any of the following):
- What we learn about human genetics will enable improvement of livestock management.
- Provides a knowledge base that is a key to understanding the structure, function, and organisation of DNA in chromosomes.
- Provides the basis for comparative studies with other organisms (e.g. for taxonomic purposes).
- Provides a greater understanding of human evolution and anthropology.
- Facilitates developments in forensics.

4. **Proteomics** is the study (including identification) of the protein products of identified genes. It relies on the knowledge gained by the HGP, but will ultimately provide the most useful information.

5. Student's own discussion. Suggestions for each issue listed in the table (pros and cons) are as follows:
- Rights of third parties:
(a) They should have the genetic information in order to make an informed decisions (about insurance premiums etc.) to the benefit of those with "favourable" genetic test results.
(b) They should be denied the information because they could use it to unfairly discriminate against people with "unfavourable" genetic test results.

- No treatment, therefore the knowledge is pointless:
(a) Although there may be no treatment initially, treatment may become available and knowledge of genetic predisposition will allow informed decisions to be made at short notice if necessary.
(b) Knowing that one has a disease and cannot do anything about it could create emotional problems for many people.

- High costs of tests:
(a) Although the costs are high, the knowledge is important to a person's health and to medical research generally and is justifiable.
(b) If costs are not met by public funds, the high costs will preclude those individuals who cannot personally afford them.

- Genetic information is hereditary:
(a) Knowledge of an inherited disease or disorder lets family members assess their risks when planning their own lives.
(b) Family members may feel forced to not have children if their risk of an inherited disorder is high.

Genome Projects (page 225)

1. (a) Yeast: 461.5 (c) Fruit fly: 93.3
(b) *E. coli*: 957.2 (d) Mouse: 12

2. The amount of (protein) coding DNA ('genes') per Mb of DNA varies greatly because different species have varying amounts of DNA in non-protein coding regions (regions traditionally not regarded as genes).

3. Determining the genomes of major crop plants, such as wheat, rice, and maize, will improve the feasibility of making appropriate, high value, and safe genetic modifications to the plants. These modifications may be for characteristics such as improved pest resistance, higher yield, lower water demand, nitrogen fixation etc. Other reasons include a better understanding of crop diseases, growth potential, and genetic resilience in the face of selective (in)breeding.

4. Sequencing the Neanderthal genome and comparison with the human genome will lead to a better understanding of human origins, and the possible function of specific genes, and the timing of genetic changes (i.e. when certain mutations arose).

A Gene That Can Tell Your Future (page 226)

1. The physical effects of Huntington's disease are shaking of hands and/or limbs and an awkward gait. More severe effects include the loss of muscle control and mental function leading to dementia.

2. The mHTT gene was discovered using information from the family history of 10,000 people. Using a probe called G8, a map of the 4th chromosome was built up and each gene sequenced. The mHTT gene was shown to be one with a trinucleotide repeat expansion.

3. HD is caused by a trinucleotide repeat expansion of the sequence CAG on the 4th chromosome. Repeats of over 35 cause the disease and the greater the number of repeats the more severe the disease. Because of the instability of the mHTT gene, the number of repeats and severity of the disease tends to increase over generations.

DNA Chips (page 227)

1. Purpose: To determine the presence or sequence of genes in a sample, and the expression or activity level of those genes.

2. (a) The gene probes making up the microarray fluoresce when cDNA binds to them (called nucleic acid hybridisation). This indicates that the RNA product has been expressed in the cell it was taken from. A quantitative amount of gene activity can be computer generated.
   (b) Reverse transcriptase makes a single-stranded copy (cDNA) of the RNA extracted from a cell.

3. (a) Genes that turned red in the microarray (2 and 24) were over-expressed and therefore the most antibiotic resistant genes from the bacteria.
   (b) New antibiotics would be designed to silence these genes that are antibiotic resistant. Alternatively, new antibiotics could also be developed to affect those bacterial genes that are not antibiotic resistant (e.g. genes 4, 17, and 22).

4. They have evolved from Southern Blotting techniques where fragmented DNA is attached to a substrate and then probed with a known gene or fragment. Many different DNA probes are incorporated into a DNA chip. Each spot on the chip has thousands-to-millions of copies of a probe and the colour of the spot allows a quantitative read-out of a particular gene's activity in a cell. Advantages include identifying which genes are expressed in a particular tissue and to what extent.

5. The information gained from the microarray could be used to identify which tissue was cancerous and to what degree the cancer was present. This would then enable specialists to advise the best treatment for a particular cancer.

DNA Profiling Using Probes (page 229)

1. (a) Suspect 1
   (b) If it had to be one of the 3 suspects then there is 100% certainty as there is a perfect match in DNA samples. If there may have been someone else involved, then there is a one in a billion chance that the suspect is not the killer (since his DNA pattern is found in one in a billion people).
   (c) The evidence (semen sample) would be contaminated with the victim's DNA. It must be shown that the victim's DNA pattern is not the same as that of the semen sample. If it was, it would invalidate the test.

2. For forensic purposes, the evidence supplied must be conclusive (beyond reasonable doubt). Blood types are not precise enough for forensic use, given that ABO blood groups are shared by many people (e.g. 49% of people of European origin are blood group **O**, while 40% are blood group **A**). Even minor blood group types (e.g. Rh, Kell, MN) are not that helpful. In contrast, the chance of another individual sharing exactly the same genetic profile with another individual is about one billion (one thousand million) to one. Note: The term **forensic** refers (broadly) to use in a court of law. Specifically here, it relates to, or denotes, the application of scientific methods and techniques to the investigation of crime.

3. The issue of sample reliability has been raised, i.e. can we be certain of the purity (non-contamination) of the suspect's tissue sample? There are also arguments over the frequency (in the population at large) of DNA markers that are tested for in the forensic analysis.

4. (a) and (b) any of the following: Screening for genetic diseases; identifying the sex of animals that are difficult to sex visually (e.g. some parrots, ostriches reared commercially); checking the pedigree of dogs, racehorses, stud cattle; checking for genetic diversity in trees in commercial forests.

Forensic Applications of DNA Profiling (page 231)

1. Lane A acts a control or calibration lane containing fragments of DNA of known length.

2. Profiles of everyone involved must be completed to compare their DNA to any DNA found at the scene and therefore eliminate (or implicate) them as suspects.

3. The alleged offender is not guilty. The alleged offender's DNA profile does not appear in the DNA collected at the crime scene nor does it appear in the DNA database. Profile E's DNA is found at the scene.

4. Each individual whale has its own DNA profile. By profiling the tissue it is possible to identify how many whales were killed by simply counting the number of different profiles. It can then be determined if the whale meat sold was from one whale or many.

Preparing a Gene for Cloning (page 232)

1. **Restriction enzymes** are used to produce the DNA fragment (often a gene) to be cloned, by isolating it from other DNA and providing it with sticky ends. The same enzymes are used to open up the vector DNA into which the DNA fragment is to be inserted.

2. (a) Introns are non-protein coding and removing them makes the gene shorter and therefore easier to insert into vectors and easier for bacteria to translate into the protein. In the case of PCR, it means large amounts of non-coding DNA are not made.
   (b) Reverse transciptase catalyses the production of a DNA strand from a strand of RNA.

3. Reverse transcriptase is found in retroviruses (such as HIV) and make a copy of DNA from the viral RNA

so that the viral genes can be integrated into (and replicated along with) the host's genome.

In Vivo Gene Cloning (page 233)

1. *In vivo* methods make it simpler to produce the protein product because the recipient of the gene (the bacterium) will express the gene as its protein product and this product can then be harvested.

2. One would not use bacteria to clone a gene if the purpose of the gene cloning was simply to amplify the DNA, e.g. for forensic or diagnostic purposes, and protein expression not was required. PCR alone is a simple automated process.

3. The gene is prepared by removal of introns. At the same time, an appropriate vector (e.g. plasmid) is isolated. Both the gene and plasmid are treated with the same restriction enzyme to produce identical sticky ends. The DNA fragments are mixed in the presence of DNA ligase and anneal (DNA ligation).

4. 2 x 24 = 48 replications in twenty four hours. Number of bacteria and therefore plasmids = 2^{48} or 2 multiplied by itself 48 times = 281,474,976,710,656 copies.

5. Recombinant colonies can be identified by their ability to grow on agar with ampicillin but not tetracycline.
   - Grow the bacteria on agar containing ampicillin. All resulting colonies must contain the plasmid.
   - Press a sterile filter paper firmly onto the surface of the agar, taking care to mark the paper's position relative to the agar plate. Press the paper onto another agar plate containing tetracycline and mark the position of the paper relative to the plate. Any colonies that do not grow on this new agar must contain the recombinant DNA (as they have been killed by tetracycline).
   - Match the position of colonies between the first and second agar plates. Those on the first plate that are missing from the second are isolated and cultured.

6. A *gfp* marker is preferable over antibiotic resistance genes because antibiotic resistance genes encourage the undesirable spread of antibiotic resistance through bacterial populations. Apart from this, a *gfp* marker system is much simpler, as the marked colonies can be quickly identified by fluorescence under UV light.

7. Viruses are used in *in vivo* cloning because they are able to insert DNA into a host's genome. Any altered DNA within them will also be inserted and then copied by the cellular machinery of the host.

Vectors in Transgenesis (page 235)

1. (a) **Transgenesis**: The transfer of genes from one organism (usually another species) to another organism (so that the recipient takes on the characteristics encoded by the foreign DNA).
   (b) **Foreign DNA**: DNA that is not part of the natural genome of a species.

2. The DNA of one organism is introduced into the genome of another (recipient) organism. The foreign DNA, when expressed, confers new properties on the recipient organism.

3. Examples include (any one):
   - A gene that provides resistance to disease.
   - A gene that confers herbicide resistance (so that weed control with herbicides will not affect the crop).
   - Gene for a character that leads to increased yield.
   - Gene that leads to a gene product that leads to increased nutritional value (e.g. higher protein content in wheat or vitamin content in rice).

4. (a) to (c) any of the following: A need to:
   - Treat genetic diseases in humans.
   - Improve production in livestock (milk, cheese, beef, mutton, wool, leather).
   - Increase pest resistance in crops and livestock.
   - Provide existing crops and livestock with (potentially useful) novel traits (e.g. timber with reduced lignin, cows milk with altered constituents).
   - Provide crops with an ability to synthesise their own fertiliser (to reduce dependence on application of agricultural fertilisers).

5. (a) **Advantages** (any two of): • Viruses are good vectors because they are adapted to gain entry into a host's cells • Viruses are very host specific with respect to infection • Viruses can integrate their DNA into that of the host.
   (b) **Disadvantage** (any of): • The host can develop a strong immune response to the viral vector (infection). In patients immune suppressed by their disorder, this severely undermines their health. • Retroviruses infect only dividing cells (uptake may be sporadic or poor). • The inserted genes may only function sporadically because they are not inserted into the chromosome.

6. The purpose of this experiment was simply to show that the technology was viable and that a transgenic animal could be produced.

Production of Human Insulin (page 237)

1. (a) High cost (extraction from tissue is expensive).
   (b) Non-human insulin (from pigs or cattle) is different enough from human insulin to cause side effects.
   (c) The extraction methods did not produce pure insulin so the insulin was often contaminated.

2. Mass production of human proteins using *E. coli* facilitates a low cost, reliable supply for consumer use. The insulin protein is free of contaminants and, because it is a human protein, the side effects of its use are minimised.

3. The insulin is synthesised as two (A and B) nucleotide sequences (corresponding to the two polypeptide chains) because a single sequence is too large to be inserted into the bacterial plasmid. Two shorter sequences are small enough to be inserted (separately) into bacterial plasmids.

4. The β-galactosidase gene in *E.coli* controls the transcription of genes, so the synthetic genes must be tied to that gene in order to be transcribed.

5. (a) Insertion of the gene: The yeast plasmid is larger and could accommodate the entire synthetic nucleotide sequence for the A and B chains as one uninterrupted sequence.
   (b) Secretion and purification: Yeast, being eukaryotic, has secretory pathways that are more similar to

humans than those of a prokaryote. Secretion from the cell of the precursor insulin molecules is thus less problematic. Purification would be simplified because removal of β-galactosidase is not required.

Golden Rice (page 240)

1. The genes for two different enzymes involved in beta carotene synthesis are taken from two different sources and inserted into the nuclear genome of a rice plant. Expression of the gene under the control of an endosperm-specific promoter results in production of beta carotene in the edible portion of the rice plant.

2. The expression of the genes is controlled by a promoter specific to the endosperm, so the genes will only be expressed in that tissue.

3. *Agrobacterium tumefaciens* is a natural plant pathogen and can transfer genes as a consequence of infecting a host plant. The tumour-inducing Ti plasmid can be modified to delete the tumour-forming gene and insert a gene for a desirable trait.

4. (a) Production and consumption of beta-carotene rich rice could alleviate or prevent diseases related to vitamin A deficiency (e.g. night blindness and susceptibility to infection as a result of low immunity). Beta carotene is a precursor to vitamin A.
   (b) Improved nutrition through GM rice will be viable only if the diet in targeted regions is also adequate with respect to fat intake. In some impoverished regions this will not be the case, as diet is inadequate across a wide range of food groups, including fat and protein.

5. (a) More grains per head, larger grains.
   (b) Faster maturation time.
   (c) Improved resistance to pests (e.g. by producing a natural toxin or thicker seed coat etc).

Xenotransplantation (page 241)

1. (a) Xenotransplants are usually immune rejected because of histocompatibility differences. Differences in organ size and shape between the donor and recipient species are also problematic and cause failure.
   (b) Genetic engineering can create pigs that are more immuno-compatible with human recipients. The GE pig cells either express human proteins on their cell surface or the fail to express the GT antigen that normally triggers immediate rejection of the xenotransplant.

2. Pig organs are a comparable size to humans, so this minimises problems associated with size and shape differences. Pigs are phylogenetically distant from humans so the risk of cross species disease transfer is minimised. Pigs are also suitable for genetic modification, which is carried out to reduce immune rejection in the recipient.

3. Immediate rejection of the xenotransplant is now prevented by the use of GE pigs that lack the GT antigen that normally triggers this.

Gene Therapy (page 242)

1. (a) The principle of gene therapy is to correct a genetic disorder of metabolism by correction, replacement, or supplementation of a faulty gene with a corrected version. **Note**: Some techniques involve culturing corrected cells *ex vivo*. Injection of corrected cells into the patient relieves the symptoms of the disorder but does cure it.
   (b) Medical areas where gene therapy might be used: Inherited genetic disorders of metabolism, cancers and other non-infectious acquired diseases, and infectious diseases (e.g. viral infections).

2. Transfection of (and correction of the genes in) **germline cells** allows the genetic changes to be inherited. **Note**: In this way, a heritable disorder can be corrected so that future generations will not carry the faulty gene(s). Transfection of **somatic cells** only corrects those cells for their lifetime.

3. **Gene amplification** is used to make multiple copies of the normal (corrective) allele.

4. GM stem cells offer longer lasting treatment because the cells will continue proliferating and the therapeutic role will continue as long as the cell line continues. Once a transformed (corrected) somatic cell has reached the end of its life, its therapeutic role ends.

Gene Delivery Systems (page 243)

1. (a) **CF symptoms**: Disruption of gland function including the pancreas, intestinal glands, biliary tree, sweat glands, and bronchial glands. Infertility occurs in males and females. Disruption of lung function produces the most obvious symptom; the accumulation of thick, sticky mucus in the lungs and associated breathing difficulties.
   (b) CF has been targeted because the majority of cases are the result of a gene defect involving the loss of only one triplet (three nucleotides). In theory, correction of this one gene should not be difficult.
   (c) Correction rate has been low (25%), and the effects of correction have been short lived and the benefits quickly reversed. These problems are related to the poor survival of the viral vector in the body and the sporadic functioning of the gene because it is not integrated into the host's (human) chromosome. Patients suffer problems with immune reaction to the vector. In one patient, treatment was fatal.

2. (a) **Vector**: Adenoviruses.
   Note: potential problems (not required): Gene may function only sporadically when not integrated into the host's chromosome. Adenoviruses have poor survival in the body and are quickly destroyed by the immune system. As a result, corrective rates are low and the effects of the corrective gene are short lived. Patients may show various adverse reactions, as a result of their immune response to the vector.
   (b) **Vector**: Liposomes
   Note: potential problems (not required): Liposomes are less efficient than viruses at transferring genes, so corrective rates are lower than for viral vectors.

3. (a) X-linked SCID is caused by a mutation to a gene on the X chromosome encoding the common gamma

chain. ADA SCID is caused by a defective gene that codes for the enzyme adenosine deaminase.
   (b) The vector used in the treatment of SCID is a gutted retrovirus (a retorvirus with its natural genetic material removed to make room for the corrective gene being transferred).

4. Gene therapy for cystic fibrosis is targeted at the lungs using either an adenovirus or a liposome delivered via the airways. SCID is treated using a retrovirus introduced to the patient's own bone marrow and the returned to the patient.

5. (a) Chance of interfering with essential gene function: When an essential gene function is affected by gene therapy in somatic cells, the individual will be affected. There may be a chance of corrective therapy in that person's lifetime. When the change affects germline cells, descendants of the treated individual have a chance to inherit the disrupted gene, so a second heritable defect is created.
   (b) Misuse of the therapy to selectively alter phenotype:
   Alteration of somatic cells to selectively alter one's phenotype is (presumably) a matter of one's own choice; it may benefit that person in their own lifetime, but will not affect subsequent generations. When these selective changes affect the germline cells, then they are heritable and the alteration is not necessarily limited to one individual. This poses the problem of genetic selection and eugenics, and all their consequent ethical dilemmas.

Vectors for Gene Therapy (page 245)

1. (a) Viruses are good vectors because they are adapted to gain entry into a host's cells and integrate their DNA into that of the host.
   (b) Viral vectors can cause problems because (two of):
   - The host can develop a strong immune response to the viral infection. In patients disadvantaged (immune suppressed) by their disorder, this could severely undermine their health.
   - Retroviruses infect only dividing cells.
   - Viruses may not survive if attacked by the host's immune system.
   - If they do not integrate into the chromosome, the inserted genes may only function sporadically.
   - The genes may integrate randomly into chromosomes and disrupt the functioning of normal genes (this occurred recently in retroviral vectors used in SCID gene therapy patients).

2. (a) If a therapeutic gene is integrated into the chromosome, it has a better chance of functioning properly in the long term, and being stable (not degraded) in the cell.
   (b) When it integrates into the host's (patient's) chromosome, the gene has the potential to disrupt normally functioning genes (see 1(b) above). **Note**: in some gene therapy trials in SCID patients, retroviral vectors integrated preferentially into currently active genes.

3. (a) Naked DNA is unstable because it is recognised as foreign and is easily degraded by the normal clean-up mechanisms occurring in the host's tissues (phagocytes etc.). Uptake by cells is inefficient and, once within the cell, the DNA is still at risk of degradation by lysosomes.
   (b) Liposomes offer greater stability because they are formulated so that they are recognised by the host's cell receptors and they target these receptors (so are more directed). They are therefore less likely to be degraded in the tissues.

Genetic Counselling (page 246)

1. **Carrier screening** would allow the parents to ascertain the risk of conceiving a child with the family genetic disorder. This information could then be used to explore alternative methods of conceiving a child that is at lower risk of inheriting the disorder.

2. (a) Huntington disease persists because those with the mutation are able to reproduce and pass on the disorder before its effects are expressed.
   (b) Presymptomatic genetic testing would allow carriers of the Huntingtin gene to make informed choices when considering starting a family.

Food for the Masses (page 247)

1. The bacterium. This bacterium uses only one enzyme to facilitate multiple reactions. It is therefore simpler to use in the production of the modified plant.

2. The gene can be isolated by first identifying the associated enzyme and its amino acid sequence. From this the mRNA sequence can be identified. The correct mRNA molecules can then be extracted from the cell and reverse transcriptase used to copy the mRNA into DNA. This can then be amplified.
   Or - Once the DNA sequence is identified, PCR primers can be produced that will anneal to the start sequences of the gene. The PCR product will be the targeted gene.
   Or The gene can be identified from its protein product (as above). This can then be cut from the chromosome using restriction enzymes and amplified.

3. *Agrobacterium*. This bacterium can transfer DNA into plants, so that the cells will contain recombinant DNA.

4. A plasmid (the *Ti* plasmid) is removed from the Agrobacterium. Using restriction enzymes the plasmid is cut and the target DNA inserted (the tumour forming gene is removed). DNA ligase is used to attach the target DNA to the plasmid. The plasmid is then replaced into the *Agrobacterium*.

5. (a) *Agrobacterium* transfers the recombinant plasmid to the cells of the target plant.
   (b) The best stage of development for transformation is while the plant is in embryonic form. In this way a larger proportion of the plant cells will be affected and take up the new DNA. This will cause a much better result in the adult plant.

6. Transformed plants can be identified if an extra gene is inserted along with the target gene. This is normally a gene for drug resistance. Plants grown on agar impregnated with the chemical will grow only if they have taken up the new DNA. Those without won't grow.

7. A large number of plants can be produced using plant tissue culture or vegetative propagation. In this way many plants can be produced, which will lead to rapid dissemination of the transgenic stock.

The Ethics of GMO Technology (page 249)

1. Plants produce pollen which has the potential to be spread in a broadcast fashion (broadcast pollination). This increases the risk that genes (e.g. for herbicide resistance) will be transferred from a GM plant to a weed or other plant. **Note**: Such gene transference has already been demonstrated between plant species. Transfer of sex cells (and therefore genes) between animals in this way does not occur; animal breeding is generally a more precise and difficult process.

2. (a) Advantage: Crop growers could spray a field with herbicide to kill weeds without harming the crop.
   (b) Problem: Herbicide resistance may be spread to weed plants by viral or bacterial vectors that infect plants. Encourages overuse of herbicide chemicals.

3. (a) Advantage: Ability to grow tropical food crops in regions that could not previously do so.
   (b) Problem: Such plants in a new environment may become pest species. Undeveloped economies that rely on tropical cash crops may suffer as a result of competition from economically strong countries.

4. (a) Advantage: Will allow regions that are poor in agricultural production to produce crops.
   (b) Problem: Such plants in a new environment may become pest species. Disturbs natural wetland habitats, probably resulting in the loss of wetland and marsh native species.

5. In any order:
   (a) Enhancing wool production in sheep (yield and/or wool quality).
   (b) Use of livestock animals as biofactories by producing useful proteins in their milk (especially cattle, but also sheep and goats).

6. The widespread use of antibiotic marker genes in food crops for human consumption or stock food may give rise to antibiotic resistant strains of pathogenic bacteria which affect humans and stock animals. Restrained use of antibiotics is now considered essential in preventing large scale development of antibiotic resistance.

7. (a) Introduces nitrogen fixing ability in non-legumes thereby reducing the need for nitrogen fertilisers.
   (b) The bacterium would prevent attack on the seeds by pathogenic bacteria and fungi.

8. **Note**: This question was not intended to imply that ethical or moral concerns are any less real or valid than biological ones. It was merely an exercise in identifying the nature of the biological concerns.
   (a) Some points for discussion are:
   - That the GM product and/or the GMO could have some unwanted harmful effect on humans or other organisms.
   - That the genetic modification would spread uncontrollably into other organisms (breeding populations of the same or different species).
   - Consumer choice is denied unless adequate labelling protocols are in place. If everything contains GM products, there is no consumer choice in this area.
   - General fear of what is not understood (fear of real or imagined consequences).
   - Objections on the grounds that it is ethically and morally wrong to tamper with the genetic make-up of an organism.
   - Generation of monopolies where large companies control the rights to seed supplies & breeding stock.

   (b) Those that pose a real biological threat are:
   - Amongst plant GMOs, the indiscriminate spread of foreign genes.
   - Unusual physiological reactions e.g. allergies, to novel proteins.
   - Some animal rights issues may be justified if genetic modification causes impaired health.

KEY TERMS: Mix and Match (page 251)

Annealing (B), Biotechnology (F), Blunt end (U), DNA chip (N), DNA ligation (V), DNA ligase (W), DNA polymerase (O), DNA sequencing (G), Forensics (J), Gel electrophoresis (Q), Gene technology (R), GMO (P), Marker gene (X), Microsatellite (M), Molecular clone (Y), PCR (H), Plasmid (I), Primer (D), Recognition site (S), Recombinant DNA (K), Restriction enzyme (E), Sticky end (T), Transformation (L), Transgenesis (Z), Vector (A), Xenotransplant (C).

Components of an Ecosystem (page 253)

1. A **community** is a naturally occurring group of organisms living together as an ecological entity. The community is the biological part of the ecosystem. The **ecosystem** includes all of the organisms (the community) and their physical environment.

2. The biotic factors are the influences that are the result of the activities of living organisms in the community whereas the abiotic (physical) factors are the influences of the non-living part of the community, e.g. climate.

3. (a) Population (c) Community
   (b) Ecosystem (d) Physical factor

Food Chains (page 254)

1. (a) The Sun.
   (b)-(d): See diagram below.

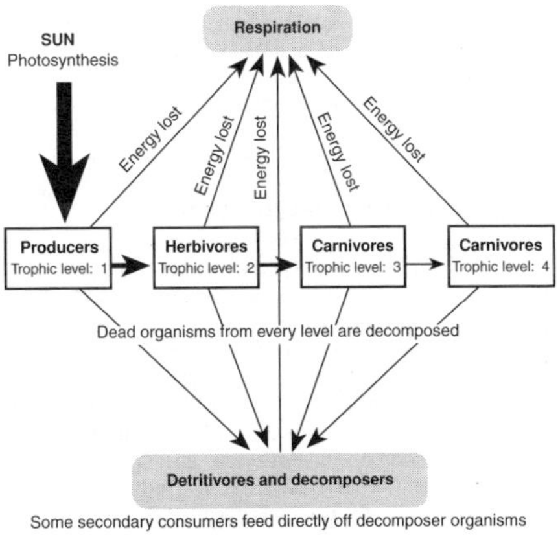

2. (a) Each successive trophic level has less energy.
   (b) Energy is lost by respiration as it is passed from

one trophic level to the next.

3. A **food chain** comprises a sequence of organisms, each of which is a source of food for the next. Food chains in ecosystems are organised according to **trophic levels**; the feeding levels that energy passes through as it proceeds through the food chain. Organisms are assigned a category according to the trophic level they occupy. Producers form the first trophic level, 1st order consumers (primary consumers) eat producers (i.e they are herbivores), 2nd order consumers (secondary consumers) eat herbivores (i.e. they are carnivores) etc. Organisms may occupy more than one trophic level depending on their diet. Detritivores and decomposers obtain energy from all other trophic levels and are therefore not assigned a trophic level.
4. The kingfisher occupies trophic level 3 or 4 at different times (depending on the prey of choice).

Energy Inputs and Outputs (page 255)

1. Producers are organisms that can manufacture organic (carbon) compounds from an inorganic source. They may be phototrophic (where the sun is the source of the energy to do this) or chemotrophic (where chemicals provide the energy). Consumers are organisms dependent on external organic compounds, which are taken in as a means of obtaining energy and/or nutrients. This group includes all animals, fungi, and parasitic flowering plants. Decomposers are organisms obtaining organic matter in solution from dead and decaying organisms by extracellular digestion. This group includes decomposer bacteria and fungi involved in decay. Note that decomposers are also consumers.
2. Decomposer bacteria produce heat. This comes from respiration.
3. By breaking down dead matter, decomposers make nutrients available to other trophic levels (especially to producers). They recycle nutrients within ecosystems and some consumers rely on them directly for food.
4. (a) Decomposers is a term for those organisms that obtain their nutrients from the extracellular breakdown of dead material whereas detritivores is a term usually reserved for organisms that obtain nutrients from ingesting dead material (typically, but not exclusively, of plant origin).
   (b) Detritivores, by directly feeding on dead material (and also defaecating), break it into smaller fragments. This increases the surface area available for decomposers to work on and thus speeds up the decomposition process.
5. (a) Excreted products are still rich in energy (urea, uric acid, ammonia, alcohol). Some egested material leaves the organism in an undigested state, e.g. the cellulose in plant material.
   (b) Cellular respiration is not completely efficient. Some energy from the break down of glucose is lost as heat energy to the environment.

Constructing a Food Web (page 257)

1. Some food chain examples as below (there are others)
   (a) Algae → zooplankton → diving beetle
   (b) Algae → zooplankton → stickleback → pike
   (c) Macrophyte → great pond snail → herbivorous water beetle → stickleback → pike
   (d) Macrophyte → carp → pike
   (e) Algae → mosquito larva → *Hydra* → dragonfly larva → carp → pike
   (f) Macrophyte → herbivorous water beetle → carp → pike
   (g) Algae → zooplankton → *Asplanchna* → leech → dragonfly larva → carp → pike
   (h) Detritus → *Paramecium* → *Asplanchna* → leech → dragonfly larva → carp → pike
   (i) Detritus → great pond snail → leech → dragonfly larva → carp → pike
   (j) Detritus → *Paramecium* → mosquito larva → *Hydra* → dragonfly larva → carp → pike
2. (a) and (b) Food web: See diagram below.

Energy Flow in an Ecosystem (page 259)

1. (a) 14 000 (b) 180 (c) 35 (d) 100
2. Solar energy
3. A. Photosynthesis
   B. Eating/feeding/ingestion

Constructing a lake foodweb:
For reasons of space, the names have been omitted from this solution but the relative positions of each organism is as presented in the workbook. Trophic levels are indicated by the letter T and the number(s) of the level(s) occupied. Note: the trophic level a species occupies will depend on the trophic position of its food items. For example, the carp occupies several different trophic levels, since it feeds on macrophytes, and on both primary and tertiary consumers. The tertiary consumers that the carp eats will also be feeding at a number of different levels, hence the complexity of food webs and the difficulty in accurately representing them in diagrams.

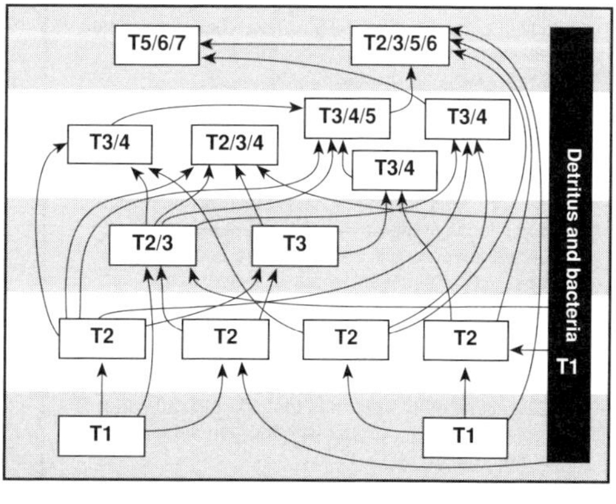

C. Respiration
D. Export (lost from this ecosystem to another)
E. Decomposers and detritivores feeding on other decomposers and detritivores
F. Radiation of heat to the atmosphere
G. Excretion/egestion/death

4. (a) 1 700 000 ÷ 7 000 000 x 100 = 24.28%
(b) It is reflected. Plants appear green because those wavelengths are not absorbed. Reflected light falls on other objects as well as back into space.

5. (a) 87 400 ÷ 1 700 000 x 100 = 5.14%
(b) 1 700 000 - 87 400 = 1 612 600 (94.86%)
(c) Most of the energy absorbed by the producers is **not** used in photosynthesis. This excess energy which is not fixed is lost as heat (although the heat loss component **before** the producer level is not usually shown on energy flow diagrams). **Note**: Some of the light energy absorbed through accessory pigments widens the spectrum that can drive photosynthesis. However, much of accessory pigment activity is associated with photoprotection; they absorb and dissipate excess light energy that would otherwise damage chlorophyll.

6. (a) 78 835 kJ
(b) 78 835 ÷ 1 700 000 x 100 = 4.64%

7. (a) Decomposers and detritivores
(b) Transport by wind or water to another ecosystem.

8. (a) Energy remains locked up in the detrital material and is not released.
(b) Geological reservoir:

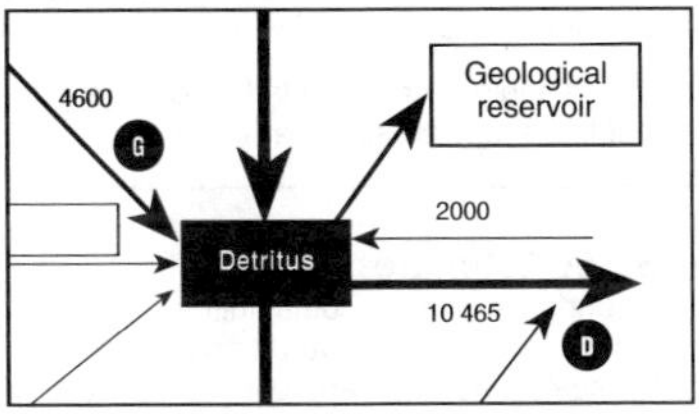

(c) **Oil** (petroleum) and **natural gas**, formed from the remains of marine plankton. **Coal** and **peat** are both of plant origin; peat is partly decomposed, and coal is fossilised.

9. (a) 87 400 → 14 000: 14 000 ÷ 87 400 x 100 = 16%
(b) 14 000 → 1600: 1600 ÷14 000 x 100 = 11.4%
(c) 1600 → 90: 90 ÷ 1600 x 100 = 5.6%

Production and Trophic Efficiency (page 261)

1. Net primary production refers to the net amount of producer biomass available per unit area to the next trophic level. Net primary productivity is the rate of producer biomass production or the producer biomass produced per area per unit time.

2. (a)- (c) and any of the following:
- Amount and availability of light for photosynthesis. This will be dependent partly on latitude and is higher in the tropics.
- Temperature; higher temperatures are generally conducive to higher productivity.
- Availability of water; photosynthesis (and therefore productivity) will be limited when water is scarce.
- Availability of nutrients; nutrient limitations will limit plant growth and lower productivity.

3. (a)-(c) any of the following:
- High diversity of grassland species contributing to ecosystem efficiencies (different tolerances and preferences so photosynthesis is maximised across a wide region).
- High root production typical of herbaceous species.
- High producer turnover because of continual cropping by herbivores so plants are always actively growing (as opposed to having a large amount of non-producing biomass like wood).
- High rates of nutrient recycling (e.g. by termites and dung beetles) so nutrient availability is not a factor in limiting productivity.
- Savanna occurs in equatorial or near equatorial latitudes so high light and temperature help to increase rates of plant photosynthesis.
- Continual supplies of nutrient from the dung of primary consumers (grazing herbivores).

4. (a) The procedure outlined only gives an estimate of NPP because you cannot easily make allowances for the plant material not collected due to consumption or death.
(b) To express standing crop in kJ m^{-2} you would need to know the energy content of the plant material (per known mass unit measured, e.g. kg). **Note**: This could be done using a calorimeter.
(c) To calculate GPP you need to know the energy lost in respiration, e.g. by measuring CO_2 loss at night.

5. (a) NPP of a particular crop can be maximised be reducing losses to pests, spraying to reduce loss of biomass to disease, maximising light penetration and nutrient uptake by keeping competing plants to a minimum (e.g. by weed control), ensuring adequate amounts of water and nutrients.
(b) Livestock productivities can be maximised using the same principles: minimising levels of disease and ensuring optimum nutrition, optimising stocking densities to reduce stress, reducing energy losses by restricting excessive movement (smaller paddocks) and providing shelter belts or indoor housing in colder weather.

6. Deserts, although often high light environments, are limited by water and nutrient availability and productivities are consequently low. By contrast, intensive horticultural land is provided with plentiful water and nutrients (applied) and crops are often kept in climate controlled environments (e.g. glasshouses) to maximise temperatures and raise carbon dioxide levels. The result is very high productivities.

Ecological Pyramids (page 263)

1. (a) Number pyramid: Numbers of individual organisms at each trophic level.
(b) Biomass pyramid: Weight (usually dry weight) of all organisms at each trophic level.
(c) Energy pyramid: Energy content of all organisms at each trophic level.

2. Biomass or energy pyramids usually more accurately reflect the energy available to the next trophic level than pyramids of numbers. Pyramids of numbers can

be misleading because a small number of producers may represent a large amount of biomass or energy.

3. Producers include the large trees. These have a large biomass and energy content per individual.

4. (a) 8690 → 142 = 8 548 kJ = 1.6%
   (b) 142 → 12 = 130 kJ = 8.5%
   (c) Energy passed on from producers to primary consumers is less than the expected 10% because a lot of energy is diverted to the decomposers.
   (d) Decomposers
   (e) In a plankton community, turnover times (generation times of organisms) are very short and there is a lot of dead material both in the water and on the bottom. This provides a rich energy source to support a large biomass of decomposers.

5. The algae are reproducing at a high rate, but are being heavily cropped by the larger biomass of zooplankton.

Primary Succession (page 265)

1. Glacial retreat, exposed slip, new volcanic island.

2. (a) Lichens and bryophytes (mosses and liverworts), as well as some hardy annual herb species, are often the first to colonise bare ground.
   (b) Chemically and physically erode the rock (making the beginnings of a soil) and add nutrients by decay.

3. Climax communities tend to have greater biodiversity and a more complex trophic structure than early successional communities. A greater diversity of community interactions buffers the system against disturbances because there are many more organisms with different ecological roles able to compensate for losses from the system.

Succession on Surtsey (page 266)

1. Surtsey was ideal as a study site for primary succession because it was an entirely new island, devoid of any soil, and was isolated from nearby influences (such as already established vegetation or urban settlements) that could accelerate the succession process.

2. Early colonisations were primarily influenced by the island's location to the south of Iceland, so the northern shores are closest to a land mass. Later colonisations were influenced buy the establishment of a gull colony at the southern end of the colony. The gulls would transport seeds and contribute to soil fertility.

3. (a) 1985.
   (b) Transported by birds.
   (c) 1985. This coincides with the establishment of the gull colony as the gulls were instrumental in dispersing seeds.

Sampling Populations (page 267)

1. We sample populations in order to gain information about their abundance and composition. Sampling is necessary because, in most cases, populations are too large to examine in total.

2. (a) Random or systematic quadrat sampling.
   (b) Random or systematic point sampling (using a net or trap).
   (c) Line transect with point sampling (from low to high altitude). If time for sampling and analysis is not constrained, a belt transect using quadrats at regular intervals would provide the most information.

3. Information about the physical environment helps to explain species distributions. Certain species are usually associated with a particular suite of physical factors (e.g. preferred exposure, temperature, humidity etc) and if these are measured and known, more information on community patterns can be gathered.

4. As the vertical distance up the trunk increases, light intensity and temperature increase and humidity declines. With these changes in physical conditions there is consequent change in the vegetation from a diverse community of shade and moisture adapted moss species, to a community comprising just one species of (hardier) tree moss and various species of lichens, i.e. species more tolerant of the microclimate of lower humidity and higher light and temperature.

Quadrat Sampling (page 269)

1. Mean number of centipedes captured per quadrat:
   Total number centipedes ÷ total number quadrats
   30 individuals ÷ 37 quadrats
   = 0.811 centipedes per quadrat

2. Number per quadrat ÷ area of each quadrat
   0.811 ÷ 0.08 = 10.1 centipedes per m^2

3. Clumped or random distribution.

4. Presence of suitable microhabitats for cover (e.g. logs, stones, leaf litter) may be scattered.

Quadrat-Based Estimates (page 270)

1. Species abundance in plant communities can be determined by using quadrats and transects, and abundance scales are often appropriate. Methods for sampling animal communities are more diverse, and density is a more common measure of abundance.

2. **Size**: Quadrat must be large enough to be representative and small enough to minimize sampling effort.

3. **Habitat heterogeneity**: Diverse habitats require more samples to be representative because they are not homogeneous.

4. (a) and (b) any two of:
- The values assigned to species on the scale are subjective and may not be consistent between users.
- An abundance scale may miss rarer species and overestimate conspicuous ones.
- The scale may be inappropriate for some habitats.
- The semi-quantitative values assigned to the categories cover a range so results will lack precision.

Sampling a Leaf Litter Population (page 271)

It must be emphasised that the actual results for this practical are not particularly important. What is of value, is learning the value and limitations of this method, preferably **before** students are asked to carry it out in a field situation. The actual results will vary, depending upon the group's agreed upon criteria for inclusion of organisms in a given quadrat (i.e. when and how an organism is counted when it is partly inside a quadrat).

Note: Some leaves are almost completely obscured by invertebrates or have other leaves on top of them.

6. Typical results for samples used are:

	Direct count	A	B	C	D
Woodlice:	89	9.5	5	13	14.5
Centipedes:	3	0	0	1	1
Springtails:	6	0	3	0	0
False scorpions:	3	1	0	1	0
Leaves:	168	29	20.5	24.5	26.5

Class results will vary depending on counting criteria.

7. Typical results for calculated density are:

	Direct count	A	B	C	D
Woodlice:	2747	1759	926	2407	2685
Centipedes:	93	0	0	185	185
Springtails:	185	0	556	0	0
False scorpions:	93	185	0	185	0
Leaves:	5185	5370	3796	4537	4907

Note: Area of 6 quadrats = $(0.03 \times 0.03) \times 6 = 0.0054\ m^2$
Area of total sample area = $0.18 \times 0.18 = 0.0324\ m^2$

8. (a) **Problems** with sampling moving organisms: Once the quadrats have been laid, the animals moving from one quadrat to another risk being counted twice. **Solutions**: Physical barriers could be placed between each quadrat (what about the invertebrates directly underneath?). The entire area could be photographed for later analysis.
   (b) Data given above. Students should be made aware of the significance of extrapolating data from a small sample. The inclusion or exclusion of single individuals may have a large effect on the density figure, particularly where the species occur in low densities. Groups could combine data to see if they get a more representative sample.

Transect Sampling (page 273)

1. (a) With belt transects of any length (10 m or more), sampling (and sample analysis) using this method is very time consuming and labour intensive.
   (b) Line transects, although quicker than belt transects, may not be representative of the community. There may be many species which are present but which do not touch the line and are not recorded.
   (c) Belt transects use a wider strip along the study area and there is much less chance that a species will not be recorded.
   (d) It is not appropriate to use transects in situations involving highly mobile organisms.

2. To test whether or not the transect sampling interval was sufficient to accurately sample the community, the sampling interval could be decreased (e.g. from a sampling interval of every 1.5 m to an interval of every 0.25 m). If no more species are detected and the trends along the transect remain the same, then the sampling interval was adequate.

3.

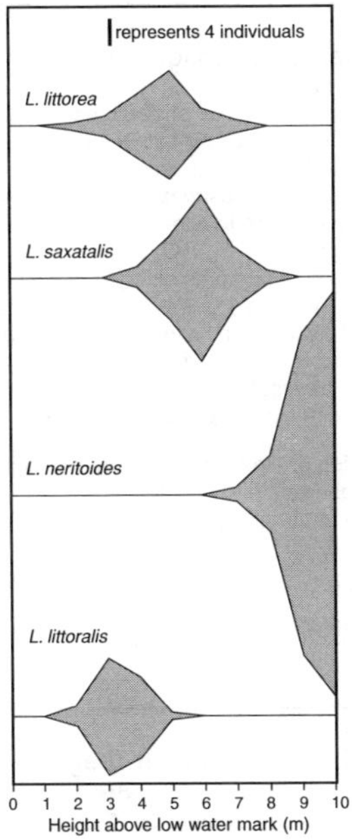

Nutrient Cycles (page 275)

1. (a) Bacteria have the ability to make conversions to and from elements and their ionic states. This gives plants and animals access to nutrients that they would otherwise not have (i.e. increases bioavailability).
   (b) Fungi decompose organic matter, returning nutrients to the soil where plants and bacteria can access them. They are also able to convert some nutrients into more readily accessible forms.
   (c) Plants are able make their own food and, when they die, add this to the soil in the form of nutrients that can be broken down and used by bacteria and fungi. They also provide browsing animals with nutrients when they are eaten.
   (d) Animals break down materials from plants, fungi and bacteria and return then to the soil with their wastes and when they die allowing the nutrients in them to re-enter the cycle.

2. The rates of decomposition is very high in the higher temperatures of tropical forests. As a result, decaying matter is processed very quickly and very little remains in the soil. Much of the carbon and other nutrients are also locked up in biomass.

3. A macronutrient is one that is required in large amounts and often needs to be replaced on a regular basis by eating or drinking. They are often needed for growth and repair of the organism. Micronutrients (trace elements) are needed in much smaller amounts and may not need to be replaced very often. However they

are often essential to the efficient operation of sensitive biochemical pathways (e.g. as enzyme cofactors).

The Nitrogen Cycle (page 276)

1. (a)-(e) any of:
- Decomposition or decay of dead organisms, to ammonia by decomposer bacteria (ammonification).
- Nitrification of ammonium ions to nitrite by nitrifying bacteria such as *Nitrosomonas* ($NH_4^+ \rightarrow NO_2^-$)
- Nitrification of nitrite to nitrate by nitrifying bacteria such as *Nitrobacter* ($NO_2^- \rightarrow NO_3^-$)
- Denitrification of nitrate to nitrogen gas by anaerobic denitrifying bacteria e.g. *Pseudomonas*n($NO_3^- \rightarrow N_{2(g)}$)
- Fixation of atmospheric nitrogen to nitrate by N fixing bacteria, e.g. *Azotobacter* and *Rhizobium* ($N_2 \rightarrow NO_3^-$)
- Fixation of atmospheric nitrogen to ammonia by nitrogen fixing cyanobacteria ($N_2 \rightarrow NH_3$)

2. (a) Oxidation of atmospheric nitrogen by lightning.
   (b) Nitrogen fixation (by bacteria).
   (c) Production of nitrogen fertiliser through the Haber process.
3. Denitrification
4. The atmosphere.
5. Nitrate.

KEY TERMS: Mix and Match (page 277)

Abiotic factor (N), Abundance (G), Belt transect (Y), Biotic factor(E), Climax community (Q), Community (I), Consumer (L), Decomposer (A), Denitrification (D), Detritivore (Z), Distribution (F), Ecological pyramid (M), Ecological succession (R), Ecosystem (H), Energy flow diagram (O), Food chain (U), Food web (W), Line transect (V), Nitrification (J), Nitrogen fixation (AA), Primaru consumer (X), Primary succession (C), Producer (P), Quadrat (B), Secondary consumer (T), Ten percent law (S), Trophic level (K).

Features of Populations (page 279)

1. (a) One of the following:
   Population growth rate: If this increases (or decreases) from one time interval to the next, it indicates that the population is probably also increasing (or decreasing). **Note**: The **intrinsic** rate of population increase (r_{max}) should be distinguished from population growth rates that account for the increasing number of individuals in the population (rN). The intrinsic population growth rate is a characteristic value for each species but rN can increase rapidly as more and more individuals add to the population increase.
   Total abundance: If this increases (or decreases) from one time interval to the next, it indicates that the population is also increasing (or decreasing).
   Mortality: If this is increasing from one time interval to the next, it indicates that the population may be decreasing (you must also account for other sources of population change).
   Birth rate & population fertility: If these increase from one time interval to the next, they indicate that the population may be increasing (you must also account for other sources of population change).
   Age structure: A population dominated by young individuals is usually increasing. A population dominated by old (especially post-reproductive) individuals is usually decreasing.
   (b) One of the following:
   Distribution: A very clumped distribution may indicate that only some parts of the environment are suitable for supporting individuals.
   Population growth and birth rates: If these are low or declining it may indicate an inability of the environment to support the population density.
   Mortality: If this are very high or increasing it *may* indicate an inability of the environment to support the present population density.

2. (a) **Measurable attributes**: Density, distribution, total abundance, sex ratios, migration (sometimes difficult). In some cases, depending on the organism, also age structure and population fertility.
   (b) **Calculated attributes**: Population growth rate, birth rate (natality) and death rate (mortality).

3. (a) Population sampling of an endangered species allows us to determine (any of): If population is growing and how fast; the population's age and sex structure (i.e. is it dominated by young or old, non-reproductive, individuals); population abundance, density, and distribution in different areas (habitat preference and suitability); sources of mortality (predation, disease, starvation etc.); population fertility. This information allows informed decisions to be made about the population's management.
   (b) Population sampling of a managed fish species allows us to determine the population growth rate. This is critical to establishing the level of fishing that can be supported by the population (the sustainable harvest) without irreversible population decline. The growth rate is calculated taking into account population abundance, and birth and death rates. Sustainable harvest can be built into the equation as one of the (controllable) sources of mortality.

Density and Distribution (page 280)

1. (a) Resources such as food and shelter are not usually spread through the environment in an even manner. Organisms will clump around these resources.
   (b) Some organisms group together for protection from the physical environment or from predators, or for the purposes of reproduction. Clumped distribution may also result from the dispersal method, especially in plants where reproduction may occur by seeds (widely dispersed) or vegetative methods.
2. Territorial behaviour whereby the establishment and demarcation of an area distributes individuals uniformly.
3. Resources are limited but distributed uniformly.
4. (a) **Clumped**: Many marine gastropods, colonial birds (seasonally), many mammals that exhibit grouping/ herd behaviour, schooling fish, colonial insects, many other invertebrates such as coral, some plants with limited dispersal.
   (b) **Random**: Weed plants with effective dispersal method, shellfish on sand or mud substrate.
   (c) **Uniform**: Territorial organisms, monoculture plantings (e.g. crops, timber plantations).

Population Regulation (page 281)

1. **Density dependent** factors, such as disease, parasitic infestation, competition, and predation have an increasing effect on population growth as the density of the population increases; their effects are exacerbated at high population densities because they are driven in part by the number of organisms present. **Density independent** factors, such as flood, fire, and drought have a controlling effect on population size and growth that is independent of the population density. The severity of the impact on the population is not correlated with the density of the population.
2. When population density is low, individuals are well spaced apart. This can reduce stress between individuals (improving the resistance to diseases) as well as making the transmission of the pathogen more difficult. Crowded populations are more susceptible to epidemics of infectious disease.
3. (a) Density dependent factor: Predation (e.g. by ladybird beetles), competition with other aphids for position on the best part of the plant to feed.
   (b) Density independent factor: Temperature (drop in temperature in autumn months in cooler climates causes the population to crash).

Population Growth (page 282)

1. (a) Mortality: Number of individuals dying per unit time (death rate).
   (b) Natality: Number of individuals born per unit time (birth rate).
   (c) Net migration rate: Net change in population size per unit time due to immigration and emigration.
2. Population growth will be constrained to a level that can be sustained by the factor that is most limiting.
3. (b) A declining population: $B + I < D + E$
   (c) An increasing population: $B + I > D + E$
4. (a) Birth rate = 14 births ÷ 100 total number of individuals x 100 % = 14% per year
   (b) Net migration rate = 2% per year
   (c) Death rate = 20% per year
   (d) Rate of population change: birth rate – death rate + net migration rate = 14 – 20 + 2 = –4% per year
   (e) The population is **declining**.
5. Limiting factors to human population growth: availability of food or land (to live or grow food), prevalence of disease and ability of public health system to prevent and treat it.

Population Growth Curves (page 283)

1. As population numbers increase, the resistance of the environment (to further population increase) increases. This constrains the population to keep to a size that the environment can support at any one time.
2. Environmental resistance refers to all the limiting factors that together act to prevent further population increase (achievement of intrinsic rate of population increase, r_{max}).
3. (a) The maximum population size (of a species) that can be supported by the environment.
   (b) The carrying capacity of an environment is determined by the availability of resources. Those that are limiting will determine the carrying capacity regardless of there being plentiful resources of other types. For example, a land area might contain enough suitable habitat to accommodate 10 breeding pairs of seed eating birds, but if nitrogen availability limits primary productivity to a level that provides enough food for only 5 breeding pairs, then nitrogen is the limiting factor determining the carrying capacity in that instance.
4. (a) A new introduction increases exponentially (or nearly so) in a new area because its niche in that environment is unexploited up to that point. Resources (food, space, shelter etc.) are plentiful and readily available. The population rapidly increases, then slows as the population encounters environmental resistance.
   (b) Population numbers would fluctuate around some relatively stable population size that equates to what the environment can support (the carrying capacity).
5. High rabbit densities can lower the carrying capacity of environments by reducing the ability of the environment to recover from the impacts of extra grazing pressure. In Britain, the grasslands have had a long history of exposure to rabbits, whose grazing pressure helped to maintain grasslands and prevent the invasion of shrubs.

The Rise and Fall of Human Populations (page 284)

1. The trend is of continual (close to exponential) growth in the human population.
2. The human population has grown because of increased crop yields and better medical treatment.This has led to a higher standard of living, better nutrition, and a lower mortality rate.
3. Local resources at Tikal and Easter Island were both used to support population growth. When these resources were over exploited, the populations crashed and the lands were abandoned. The early history of these examples tends to mirror what appears to be currently happening on a global scale. This helps us understand the effects of depleted resources on populations whose livelihoods are based on those resources and what can be done to prevent similar events happening again.

Species Interactions (page 285)

1. (a) **Mutualism** between a ruminant and its gut microflora: In this relationship, both parties benefit (in this case, more than two species are involved, as several microbial species are mutualistic with the ruminant). Volatile fatty acids, released as a result of microbial digestion of cellulose, provide a source of energy for the ruminant (e.g. cow, goat, sheep, deer). The microbes themselves are also digested and this provides protein. The microbes (usually a species specific combination of bacteria and ciliates) gain an oxygen free, nutrient rich environment at the optimum growing temperature.
   (b) **Commensalism** between shark and remora: In this relationship, the commensal (the remora) benefits by being transported in relative safety with very little energy cost to itself. The shark (various species

have commensal remoras) is neither benefitted nor disadvantaged by the remora's presence.

(c) **Parasitism** between tapeworm and humans: In this relationship, the tapeworm parasite (*Taenia solium*) gains by having a safe, equable environment in which to live and produce proglottids (reproductive segments), and by having a readily available supply of nutrients from the digested slurry in the host's gut. Even the proglottids are specialised for the selective absorption of digested food. The human host is harmed by the loss of nutrients to the parasite, and by gut irritation and potential infection.

(d) **Parasitism** between a cat flea and its host: In this relationship, the flea (*Ctenocephalides* spp.) is the parasite and gains by having a relatively safe environment at the right temperature in which to live and produce eggs, and by having a readily available supply of nutrients in the form of the cat's blood. The cat host (*Felis domestica*) is harmed to an extent by blood loss, but more by skin irritation and infection (including flea allergy dermatitis), and by the transmission of other parasites, such as tapeworms, which are transmitted by the flea.

2. Interactions:

	B	Description
(a)	+	Both species benefit.
(b)	0	Species A benefits, no effect on species B.
(c)	+	Species A (the host) is harmed, species B (the parasite) benefits.
(d)	–	No effect on species A, species B is harmed.
(e)	+	Species A (prey) is harmed, species B (the predator) benefits.
(f)	–	Both species (competitors) are harmed.
(g)	–	Species A (herbivore) benefits, species B (plant) is harmed.
(h)	–	Species A benefits, species B is harmed. Species A is unaffected, species B is harmed.

3. Identifying examples of species interactions:

Term	A	B
(b) Exploitation	+	–
(c) Antibiosis (or amensalism)	0	–
(d) Competition	–	–
(e) Commensalism	+	0
(f) Mutualism	+	+

Intraspecific Competition (page 287)

1. (a) **Individual growth rate**: Intraspecific competition may reduce individual growth rate when there are insufficient resources for all individuals (Examples: tadpoles, *Daphnia*, many mammals with large litters). **Note**: Individuals compete for limited resources and growth is limited in those individuals that do not get access to sufficient food.
   (b) **Population growth rate**: Intraspecific competition reduces population growth rate. Examples as above. **Note**: Competition intensifies with increasing population size and, at carrying capacity, the rate of population increase slows to zero.
   (c) **Final population size**: Intraspecific competition will limit population size to a level that can be supported by the carrying capacity of the environment. **Note**: In territorial species, this will be determined by the number of suitable territories that can be supported.

2. (a) They reduce their individual growth rate and take longer to reach the size for metamorphosis.
   (b) Density dependent.
   (c) The results of this tank experiment are unlikely to represent a real situation in that the tank tadpoles are not subject to normal sources of mortality and there is no indication of long term survivability (of the growth retarded tadpoles). **Note**: At high densities, many tadpoles would fail to reproduce and this would naturally limit population growth (and size) in the longer term.

3. Reduce intensity of intraspecific competition by:
   (a) Establishing hierarchies within a social group to give orderly access to resources.
   (b) Establishing territories to defend the resource within a specified area.

4. (a) Carrying capacity might decline as a result of unfavourable climatic events (drought, flood etc.) or loss of a major primary producer (plant species).
   (b) Final population size would be smaller (relative to what it was when carrying capacity was higher).

5. **Territoriality** is a common consequence of intraspecific competition in mammals and birds. In any habitat, resources are limited and only those with sufficient resources will be able to breed. This is especially the case with mammals and birds, where the costs of reproduction to the individual are high relative to some other taxa. Even though energy must be used in establishing and maintaining a territory, territoriality is energy efficient in the longer term because it gives the breeding pair relatively unchallenged access to resources. As is shown in the territory maps of golden eagles and great tits, territories space individuals apart and reduce intraspecific interactions. The size of the territory is related to the resources available within the defended area; larger territories are required when resources are poorer or widely dispersed. As is shown by the great tit example, when territory owners are removed, their areas are quickly occupied by birds previously displaced by competition.

Interspecific Competition (page 289)

1. The two species have similar niche requirements (similar habitats and foods). Red squirrels once occupied a much larger range than currently. This range has contracted steadily since the introduction of the greys. The circumstantial evidence points to the reds being displaced by the greys.

2. The greys have not completely displaced the reds. In areas of suitable coniferous habitat, the reds have maintained their numbers. In some places the two species coexist. **Note**: It has been suggested that the reds are primarily coniferous dwellers and extended their range into deciduous woodland habitat in the absence of competition.

3. Habitat management allows more effective long term population management *in-situ* (preferable because the genetic diversity of species is generally maintained better in the wild). Reds clearly can hold their own in competition with greys, provided they have sufficient resources. **Enhancing the habitat** preferred by the reds (through preservation and tree planting), assists their success. Providing **extra suitable food plants** also enables the reds to increase their breeding success and maintain their weight through winter (thus entering the breeding season in better condition).

4. Other conservation strategies to aid red squirrel populations could include (any of): Captive breeding and release of reds into areas where they have been displaced, control/cull of grey squirrels (particularly in habitats suitable for reds), transfer of reds from regions where populations are successful to other regions of suitable habitat, supplementary feeding prior to the breeding season, public education to encourage red squirrels over greys.

5. (a) A represents the **realised niche** of *Chthamalus*.
   (b) When *Balanus* is removed from the lower shore, the range of *Chthalamus* extends into areas previously occupied by the *Balanus*; *Balanus* normally excludes *Chthamalus* from the lower shore.

6. Features will depend on the example chosen. Typical examples for two species that are proving to be invasive in many countries worldwide are described:
   (a) **Mallard duck** (*Anas platyrhynchos*):
   - Clutch size is relatively large compared with many other duck species.
   - Mallards are sexually aggressive and are capable of interbreeding with several native duck species where their ranges come to overlap (grey ducks in New Zealand, American black duck, the Florida mottled duck, and the endangered Hawaiian duck).
   - Mallards bully native duck species in competition for food and nest sites.
   - Mallards are adaptable in different environments.

   (b) **Mosquito fish** (*Gambusia affinis*):
   - Prolific breeders in many diverse environments.
   - Aggressive competitors for food.
   - Generalist feeders, and will prey on the eggs and larvae of native fish and frogs.
   - Reproductive strategies tuned to maximizing reproductive output. Females are able to store sperm for extended periods and colonise environments without needing to meet a mate there.

Niche Differentiation (page 291)

1. (a) Different species may exploit different microhabitats within the ecosystem (e.g. tree trunks, leaf litter, lower or upper canopy).
   (b) Different species may exploit the same resources but at different times of the day or year.

2. Competition is avoided by the birds exploiting slightly different parts of the eucalypt habitat, with the birds feeding in different ways and/or on different food types.

3. Each damselfish exploits different parts of the reef crest and slopes as well as feeding on different food supplies and/or at different times of the day.

Predator-Prey Interactions (page 292)

1. (a) Usually between about 3 and 7 years (especially for pronounced peaks), although sometimes as great as a full 10 year cycle. Note that the peaks often appear to be superimposed or the lynx peaks appear to be ahead of the hare peaks; the lynx are responding to the earlier peaks in hare abundance.
   (b) Lynx are top predators, with longer reproductive times and generation times than hares. When the hare populations increase there is a considerable time delay before this increase in available food is translated into higher population growth rates in lynx (birth rates must increase, usually mortality rates must also fall). Likewise, a fall in hare numbers takes some time to be registered by a decline in lynx population growth rate.

2. Hares are the principal food item for lynx in this system; there is little opportunity for prey switching (few alternative prey). The lynx cycles follow those of the hares closely with a similar periodicity.

3. (a) When the supply of palatable food declines, birth rates decline (adults are less well nourished and litters are smaller) and the mortality rate increases (more deaths due to starvation and disease as a result of malnutrition). **Note**: Population growth rates depend on both birth and death rates: ($r = b–d$). When natality declines and mortality increases, r becomes negative and the population declines.
   (b) High mortality (losses from the population) can be sustained by species such as rodents and lagomorphs as long as they can maintain their intrinsically high birth rates. Declines in palatable food adversely affects their ability to do this.

Predator-Prey Strategies (page 293)

1. In advertising the fact that they are unpalatable, predators quickly learn to associate the colouration with distastefulness. When seen, poisonous species are not mistaken for palatable species and they are left alone.

2. Deceptive markings, such as fake eyes can momentarily, deceive predators into thinking that they are faced with a larger animal than is really the case. This may give time for the prey to escape or may result in the predator attacking a non-vital part of the prey.

3. Freezing, i.e. lying low to the ground and remaining very still can enable a prey species to avoid detection.

4. Active concealment from view (such as in a burrowing animal, e.g. rabbit, earthworm); rolling into a ball to expose prickles (hedgehog); erecting spines (porcupine), spraying noxious fluid (e.g. vegetable bug).

5. (a) and (b) any two of the following:
   - Cooperative (group) hunting in pelicans, lions.
   - Stealth, lying in wait for an ambush (angler fish).
   - Tool use in chimpanzees, otters.

6. **Batesian mimicry** describes the situation when a harmless species mimics the colouration and behaviour of a poisonous species. The mimic benefits from this because predators universally avoid attacking animals with the same warning colouration, poisonous or not. Generally the poisonous species is unaffected by the mimicry, but for this strategy to be successful, mimics should not outnumber poisonous individuals. In contrast, **Müllerian mimicry** describes the tendency of poisonous species to resemble each other. Mullerian mimicry benefits the mimicking species involved because they each reinforce the warning effect of their colouration. Predators will quickly learn to avoid all animals sharing the same colouration.

7. This question should test the student's comprehension of the evolution of predator/prey strategies, i.e. how could toxicity evolve if the prey species must be eaten in order for a predator to learn avoidance?
   (a) If a toxic species was 'mouthed' by a predator, but not killed, the toxic species could still survive to

reproduce and the predator would have learned.

(b) If the evolution of the toxicity was altruistic in that individuals die so that predators learn to avoid others of the same species. **Note**: Many toxic species are highly toxic, so that predators have an immediate reaction to contact with them. This reinforces the 'message' much more quickly than if the toxicity was weak or delayed.

Conservation and Sustainability (page 295)

1. Conservation refers to the management of a resource so that it is maintained into the future. The resource may be a living or mineral system and may focus on the efficient use of a non-renewable resource or the managed use of a living system. Sustainability refers to the idea of using resources within the capacity of the environment and the eventual replacement of what has been used. It can be viewed as a subset of conservation, mainly focusing on living systems.

2. Conservation emphasises system management whereas preservation aims to protect through isolation. Conservation uses active management to improve or restore the environment or to allow the use of a resource sustainably. Preservation may work in areas where human activity has yet to make an impact and is isolated enough that access to it is naturally restricted.

3. Societies build economies, which require resources in ever-increasing amounts as they grow. The rate of societal and economic growth may be greater than the rate of resource replenishment and, if so, the environment will suffer. In order for the environment to flourish, there must be a balance met between the growth of society, economic gains, and the environmental systems and resources affected or used.

Ecotourism in the Galápagos (page 296)

1. **Benefits of ecotourism**:
- Greater economic activity and better economic growth as a result of more jobs in the tourist industry.
- Greater local and global environmental awareness.
- Development of support services for conservation.

Disadvantages of ecotourism:
- Environmental disturbance by tourists.
- Increase in rubbish, and strain on resources in providing tourist services.
- Diversion of tourist dollars from the local economy.
- Risks of alien species invading with more sea traffic.
- Restrictions on traditional income sources, e.g. fishing.

2. (a) Increased tourist traffic increases the risks of habitat disturbance and may directly threaten some species if they are in vulnerable areas.

(b) A higher local population increases puts greater pressure on park boundaries and increases the risks associated with pollution and rubbish disposal, both of which will directly and indirectly affect flora and fauna. Fish stocks may benefit though as a result of tighter regulations on local fishing activity.

(c) Improvements in National Park services have enabled the funding of restoration projects on a number of islands, including the removal of feral pigs and goats. This has directly benefited native biota, allowing vegetation regeneration and better survival of native animal species,

(d) Tourism in the Galápagos is highly restricted with guides accompanying all tourist excursions. Their input has helped to protect the native species from tourist pressure and made people more environmentally aware, so they think carefully about the impact of their activities. Education at the local level helps people to understand how they can benefit (environmentally and economically) from conservation of the islands. These aspects help to raise the profile of the environment and the biota benefit as a consequence of that.

Sustainable Forestry (page 297)

1. (a) Coppicing: Coppicing is low-impact method of producing wood for harvest, which preserves a rich diversity of woodland species and is sustainable in the long term. However, it is a low volume method and the timber is not suitable for all uses. It is also skilled and labour intensive work and, if not carried out properly, has detrimental effects on diversity and forest structure.

(b) Strip cutting clears out a forest for harvest in strips and has the advantage that it produces relatively high volume of timber suitable for a wide range of uses while leaving enough border forest to enable rapid recovery of cleared land. It is also a low effort for return method and has a relatively low impact on the environment and on biodiversity. Most disadvantages come from the infrastructure required to carry out the forestry (roads etc) and the constraint of regeneration time (so for slow growing species it is not suitable).

(c) Clear cutting is a high volume forestry method with significant detrimental impacts on the environment (e.g. high soil erosion, habitat destruction, reduced biodiversity). The forest requires replanting and, if suitable at all, clear cutting should be restricted to fast growing plantation forests.

(d) Selective logging is a medium volume supplier of timber, but causes a moderate amount of environmental damage, which depends to an extent on how much infrastructure and machinery are associated with extracting the timber. Effects on biodiversity are usually minimal, and can be sustainable if properly managed to retain the original forest composition.

2. (a) Commercial plantations: Clear cutting.
(b) Traditional woodland: Coppicing.
(c) Second growth: Strip cutting or selective logging.

3. The student's own opinion is important here and should be qualified. Given unlimited resources, coppicing provides long term sustainability, with volume supplied from a mix of selective logging and strip cutting in second growth and plantation forests. Logging of old growth forests should never be considered sustainable.

4. Properly coppiced woodlands provide a regular timber supply and maintain an open canopy that encourages a rich understorey and faunal diversity. If a previously coppiced woodland is allowed to deteriorate without management, it becomes tall and overshaded, yet lacking the characteristics of an old growth forest. Biodiversity declines markedly. These are strong arguments for managing coppiced lands as a long term resource.

Plant Responses (page 300)

1. Light (including the light/dark cycle), gravity, temperature, touch, chemicals. These stimuli are important to plant growth and development.
2. Appropriate responses to environmental stimuli enable the plant to synchronise its daily cycles and seasonally important events, such as germination, with environmental cues. Appropriate responses enhance survival in different environments.
3. (a) Low soil water: Closing of stomata.
   (b) Falling autumn air temperature: Leaf fall, dormancy.
   (c) High wind: Closing of stomata, leaf closure (nastic response) in some plants.
   (d) Browsing animals: Leaf closure (nastic response).
   (e) Low night temperature: Closing of flowers.

Responses to Temperature in Plants (page 301)

1. (a) Dormancy: A condition induced by cold and/or shorter days and typified by extremely low metabolic rate and a suspension of growth and development.
   (b) Flowering: Some plants will only flower after the plant has been exposed to a period of low temperatures.
   (c) Germination: The seeds of some plants will only germinate after exposure to the appropriate period of low temperature (stratification). In some Australian species, the seeds must be exposed to the intense heat of a bushfire before germinating.
2. Vernalisation ensures the plant will flower during the warm weather (springtime) when the chances of successful pollination and fruit set are higher. The necessity of a **prolonged** exposure to cold ensures the plant does not "mistake' transient environmental cues.
3. Evergreens already have leaves ready to photosynthesise and channel energy into seed production during a short growing season. Their lower productivity in these regions is not sufficient to compensate for leaf loss and they must retain their leaves. In contrast, deciduous trees take much longer to regain their leafed status before producing flowers.
4. (a) Over a twelve hour period the tulip flower will open in the morning and close in the afternoon (and remain closed until the following morning).
   (b) Closing the flower during the night reduces water loss as well as reducing the likelihood that the nectary will be plundered by non-pollinating insects.

Nastic Responses (page 302)

1. – Closing the leaf makes it less attractive to grazers (especially if thorns are exposed), and less of the plant is likely to be eaten.
   – Drooping of the plant exposes less leaf surface area for evaporative loss of water during windy periods.
2. Disturbance to the leaflets is transmitted as a surface membrane potential to the cells at the base of the leaflets (pulvini). In response to the change in membrane potential, potassium ions are pumped out of the cytoplasm of the cells. Water follows osmotically, causing a sudden loss of turgor in the cells supporting the leaf(let) bases. **Note**: In the leaflets, turgor loss occurs on the upper surface of the pulvinus (leaflet folds up). In the entire leaf, turgor loss occurs on the lower surface of the pulvinus (leaf droops down).
3. During daylight, the leaves are maximally spread for light capture. At night the leaves fold down. There is no light capture and water is conserved by a lowered leaf.

Photoperiodism (page 303)

1. Light induced responses involving phytochrome (a and b any two of): Seed germination, leaf growth, flowering (long day plants), chlorophyll synthesis.
2. **Phytochrome** is a photosensitive pigment which changes from the inactive form to the active form on absorption of light. The plant measures daylength by the amount of phytochrome of each form present.
3. (a) Day length (perhaps more importantly, night length).
   (b) Any one of: (1) Flowering at the same time ensures that other flowers will be available to provide/receive pollen. (2) Synchronisation with periods of high insect activity may assist pollination.
4. Environmental cues for triggering and breaking **dormancy** include: Decreasing day length (short days); long, cold nights; dry, nitrogen deficient soils. The necessity of exposure to cold to break dormancy ensures the plant does not "mistake' transient environmental cues.
5. **Dormancy** (arrested growth and metabolism) occurs when conditions for plant growth and survival are poor (such as occurs in the winters of temperate regions). Dormancy allows survival over the inclement period. **Vernalisation** (the low temperature stimulation of flowering) is adaptive in temperate regions because, after a relatively long period of intense cold, a period of warmth indicates that the winter has passed and the new growing period has begun.
6. (a) Short-day plants: Flower only when the day length is short (average: 10 h).
   (b) Long-day plants: Flower only when the day length exceeds a certain minimum value (average: 14 h).
7. Short-day plants are really long night plants, requiring a night length of more than a minimum value. In the experiment outlined, a short-day plant failed to flower when a long night was interrupted by a short period of light (the plant interpreted this as a short night irrespective of the short day prior to it).

Tropisms and Growth Responses (page 305)

1. (a) Positive chemotropism
   (b) Negative gravitropism
   (c) Positive hydrotropism
   (d) Positive phototropism
   (e) Positive gravitropism
   (f) Positive thigmomorphogenesis (*alt.* thigmotropism)
2. A **tropism** is a growth movement in response to an environmental stimulus, where the direction of the growth response is determined by stimulus direction. Unlike a tropism, the direction of a **nastic response** is independent of the stimulus direction. Nasties are usually quite rapid, often reversible movements. Tropisms are usually slower growth responses.
3. (a) Enables roots to turn and grow down into the soil

(where they obtain moisture and nutrients).
(b) Enables coleoptiles to turn up and grow towards the sunlight (necessary for food manufacture).
(c) Enables the plant to clamber upwards and grow toward the light instead of possibly becoming smothered by more upright plants.
(d) Enables pollen tube to locate the micropyle of the embryo sac, and sperm nuclei to fertilise the egg.

Transport and Effects of Auxins (page 306)

1. (a) The growing leaves of the apical bud synthesise auxin in concentrations high enough to suppress the growth of the buds below. Consequently, the main shoot grows more vigorously than the lateral shoots.
(b) Auxin is a strong promoter of stem elongation and promotes the differentiation of stem tissue.
(c) Auxin is transported from the tips of the stems and roots to the vascular cambium at other regions of the plant where it promotes cell enlargement and differentiation.

2. Pruning removes the primary source of auxin synthesis and so also the suppressing effect of the apical shoot. Consequently, the lateral shoot growth increases.

3. There are gradients in auxin concentration as a result of growth and transport from source to site of action and this contributes to differential responses in different tissues. In addition, auxin's effect can be different in the presence of other plant hormones. For example the effect of auxin on stem length is stronger if gibberellins are present.

Investigating Phototropism (page 307)

1. (a) Hormone: auxin.
(b) Response: positive phototropism.
(c) **Point A**: Cells stay short. **Point B**: Cells elongate.
(d) Side B
(e)

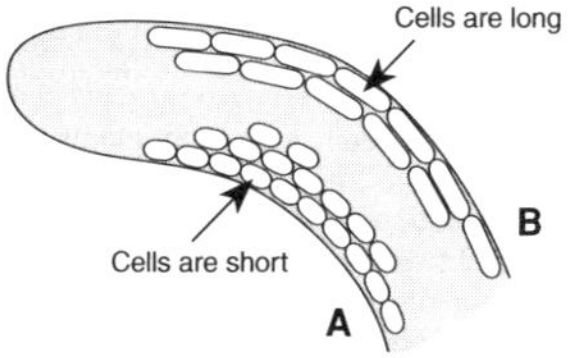

2. The hormone is produced in the shoot tip. The light initiates the response.

3. **Plant A**: The plant will exhibit phototropism and bend towards the sun.
Plant B: The plant will exhibit no phototropic behaviour and will not bend.

Investigating Gravitropism (page 308)

1. (a) In shoots, more auxin accumulates on the lower side of the shoot. In response to higher auxin levels here, the cells on the lower side of the stem elongate and the shoot tip turns up.
(b) In roots, the accumulation of auxin on the lower side inhibits elongation (since this is the response of roots to high auxin). The cells on the upper side therefore elongate more than those on the lower side and the root tip turns down.

2. (a) Approximately 10^{-3} mg l^{-1}
(b) Stem growth is promoted.

3. (a) Stems: A negative geotropic response ensures shoots turn up towards the light (important when light may be absent as when buried deeply in soil).
(b) Roots: Positive geotropism ensures roots turn down into the soil so that they can begin obtaining the water and minerals required for continued growth.

Apical Dominance, Bolting, and Leaf Loss (page 309)

1. **Auxins** in the growing leaves of the apical bud are synthesised in concentrations high enough to suppress the growth of the buds below. Consequently, the main shoot grows more vigorously than the lateral shoots.

2. **Gibberellins** are strong promoters of elongation in stems by stimulating both cell division and cell elongation. In seeds, gibberellins are responsible for breaking dormancy and stimulating the growth of the embryo and emergence of the seedling.

3. (a) Auxin is produced in the growth regions of young plants (e.g. apical tip). If the apical tip of a young seedling remains intact, no lateral growth occurs. If the apical tip is removed, there is lateral growth. Conclusion: the presence of auxin in the apical tip of young seedlings inhibits lateral growth.
(b) Differences in stem length are observed between two groups of plants grown under the same conditions, but where one group has had gibberellin applied and the other has not. The group which has had gibberellin exposure has longer stem lengths than the group with no gibberellin exposure. Conclusion: Gibberellin promotes stem elongation.

4. (a) Auxin (IAA) and ethylene.
(b) The presence of auxin in the leaf inhibits leaf abscission. However, as the leaf ages auxin levels fall and the leaf becomes more sensitive to the effects of ethylene. Ethylene promotes the production of enzymes (e.g. cellulase) which break down the cell wall in the separation layer of the petiole. This results in leaf abscission.

Plant Hormones and Applications (page 311)

1. (a) **Gibberellins**: any one of the following:
Flowering: Stimulates flowering in some plants.
Stem: Cell division and elongation. Can cause spectacular stem elongation in some plants.
Seeds: Breaks seed dormancy in many plants, and can break winter dormancy of plant.
General: Delays onset of senescence.
(b) **Cytokinins**: any one of the following:
General: Promotes cell division and differentiation. Promotes lateral bud development. Keeps shoot and root growth in balance. Inhibits leaf abscission and senescence. Sprayed on cut flowers it stops ageing. Involved in seed germination in some plants.
(c) **Ethene (ethylene)**: any one of the following:
Abscission: Promotes abscission (dropping off) of leaves, flowers, fruits.
Fruit: Promotes fruit ripening.
(d) **Abscisic acid**: any one of the following:

Leaf stomata: Causes stomatal closing in response to water stress, limiting water loss.
Abscission: Promotes leaf ageing and abscission.
Seeds: Induces dormancy in seeds.

2. (a) The growing leaves of the apical bud synthesise auxin in concentrations high enough to suppress the growth of the buds below. Consequently, the main shoot grows more vigorously than the lateral shoots.
   (b) Auxin is a strong promoter of stem elongation and promotes the differentiation of stem tissue.
   (c) Auxin is transported from the tips of the stems and roots to the vascular cambium at other regions of the plant where it promotes cell enlargement and differentiation.

3. Pruning removes the primary source of auxin synthesis and so also the suppressing effect of the apical shoot. Consequently, the lateral shoot growth increases.

4. (a) Auxins (IAA), in the form of rooting powders, applied to cuttings will promote root growth (controls the differentiation of tissues).
   (b) Ethene levels in a storage facility can be raised to induce fruit ripening.
   (c) Gibberellins can be applied to break the dormancy of seeds and buds and promote germination.
   (d) Application of abscisic acid (ABA) to seeds will promote seed dormancy. Note that no single substance is involved in inducing dormancy: rather the dormancy is controlled by the interaction of growth inhibitors (ABA) and growth promoters (gibberellins, cytokinins, and ethene).

5. (a) Auxin (IAA), gibberellins
   (b) Ethene, abscisic acid (ABA)

The Mammalian Nervous System (page 316)

1. (a) **Sensory**: Reception of internal and external stimuli.
   (b) **Integrative**: Interpretation of sensory messages.
   (c) **Motor**: Initiation and coordination of an appropriate response to the sensory input.

2. (a) **CNS**: Brain and spinal cord. The brain has ultimate control of almost all body activities (except simple spinal reflexes). The spinal cord interprets simple reflexes and relays impulses to and from the brain.
   (b) **PNS**: All nerves and sensory receptors outside the CNS. Divided into sensory and motor divisions. The motor division controls both voluntary (somatic) and involuntary (autonomic) responses. Regulates sensory reception, relays impulses to the CNS, brings about the motor response.

3. Separation of the motor division of the PNS into somatic and autonomic divisions allows essential functions to occur without conscious involvement. The conscious part of the brain is then not overwhelmed by having to coordinate every motor response. Overall, this improves efficiency of motor function.

The Autonomic Nervous System (page 317)

1. (a) **Sympathetic** NS: Fibres originate from the spinal cord in thoracic and lumbar regions. Preganglionic fibres are short and release acetylcholine. Postganglionic fibres are long and usually liberate noradrenaline.
   (b) **Parasympathetic** NS: Fibres originate from the brainstem and the sacral region of the spinal cord. Preganglionic fibres are long and postganglionic fibres are very short. All parasympathetic fibres (pre- and postganglionic) are cholinergic and liberate acetylcholine.

2. (a) The sympathetic division of the ANS is more active when the body is preparing for action ('fight or flight') while the parasympathetic division is more active in conserving energy and replenishing energy reserves ('feed or breed' or 'rest and digest'). In general, the sympathetic NS stimulates where the parasympathetic inhibits and vice versa.
   (b) Most sympathetic postganglionic nerves release noradrenaline which enters the bloodstream and is deactivated relatively slowly. In contrast, parasympathetic nerves release acetylcholine which is rapidly deactivated at the synapse with short-lived localised effects.

3. Autonomic nervous system controls visceral motor functions through reflex activity. Examples:

   Pupil reflex:
   Cranial reflex to light. Stimulation of the eye by bright light causes reflex constriction of the pupil mediated through the parasympathetic nervous system.

   Control of heart rate:
   Increase in arterial pressure causes reflex stimulation of the cardioinhibitory centre through the parasympathetic division, slowing heart rate and decreasing arterial BP to normal. If BP falls, reflex acceleration of the heart takes place: the baroreceptors do not stimulate the cardioinhibitory centre, and the accelerator centre (sympathetic) is free to dominate. A similar reflex (the Bainbridge or right heart reflex) operates in response to increased venous return. Increased return of blood to the heart causes reflex stimulation of the accelerator centre, causing heart rate to increase (sympathetic).

4. Bladder emptying is under reflex control and is stimulated by stretching of the bladder wall. Stretching causes both a conscious desire to urinate and an unconscious reflex contraction of the bladder wall and relaxation of the internal urethral sphincter. The conscious part of the brain also sends impulses to relax the external urethral sphincter. Because both conscious and unconscious controls are involved, urination can be voluntarily stopped and started at will (**recognition** of and response to the cues for bladder emptying develop around two years of age).

5. A sudden decrease in blood pressure would result in the sympathetic NS increasing the constriction of the coronary blood vessels and subsequent increase in the rate and force of contraction of the heart. As a result, blood pressure would rise.

6. Inhalation of the drug results in dilation of the bronchioles (airways) in the lungs and the patient is able to breathe more easily.

The Human Brain (page 319)

1. (a) Breathing/heartbeat: brainstem (medulla)
   (b) Memory/emotion: cerebrum
   (c) Posture/balance: cerebellum
   (d) Autonomic functions: hypothalamus
   (e) Visual processing: occipital lobe
   (f) Body temperature: hypothalamus
   (g) Language: motor and sensory speech areas
   (h) Muscular contraction: primary motor area

2. The brain is protected against physical damage and infection by the bony skull, by the meninges overlying the delicate brain tissue, and by the fluid-filled ventricles, which absorb shocks and deliver nutritive substances (via cerebrospinal fluid) to the brain tissue. The blood-brain barrier formed by the endothelial tight junctions of capillaries surrounding the brain is also the main protection against toxins and infection as microbes and many large molecules cannot cross it.

3. The brain stem is structurally continuous with the spinal cord. It is a relay centre and the nerve connections of the motor and sensory systems from the rest of the brain to the body pass through it. It regulates many autonomic functions including heartbeat, breathing, and coughing and vomiting reflexes.

4. The hypothalamus is connected with many parts of the central nervous system, including the brainstem, the limbic system and the cerebral cortex It also synthesises and secretes neurohormones, most of which acts as releasing hormones to stimulate or inhibit the secretion of pituitary hormones. In this way, the hypothalamus links the CNS with endocrine activity, receiving neural input and effecting it as an endocrine (hormonal) response.

The Mechanics of Movement (page 321)

1. (a) Prime mover: the muscle primarily responsible for the movement.
   (b) Antagonist: the muscle that opposes the prime mover. i.e. relaxes when prime mover contracts. Its action can be protective in preventing over-stretching of the prime mover during contraction.
   (c) Synergist: assists the prime mover by fine-tuning the direction of limb movement.

2. Muscles can only contract and relax, therefore they can only pull on a bone; they cannot push it. To produce movement, two muscles must act as **antagonistic** pairs to move a bone to and from different positions.

3. Muscles have an origin on one (less moveable) bone and an insertion on another (more moveable) bone. When the muscle contracts across the joint connecting the two bones, the insertion moves towards the origin, therefore moving the limb. To raise a limb, the flexor (prime mover in this case) contracts pulling the limb bone up (extensor/antagonist relaxed). To lower the limb, the extensor contracts, pulling the limb down (flexor relaxed).

4. Bones are rigid and can only move at joints where they come together. The degree of movement allowed depends the type of joint. The bones of the limbs, which need to be freely moveable are connected by synovial joints. Body parts where movement is not desirable, such as the joints of the skull, are largely rigid.

5. (a) Radius (radial tuberosity)
   (b) Ulna
   (c) Triceps
   (d) Rotation of ulna and radius

6. (a) Elbow extension
   (b) Triceps

7. (a) Nodding head = flexion and extension
   (b) Hitching a ride = abduction

Voluntary Muscle Structure and Function (page 323)

1. The neuromuscular junction is the synapse of the axon terminal of a motor neurone with the motor end plate. The motor end plate is the region of muscle fibre (cell) plasma membrane responsible for initiating action potentials, which are then conducted to all the myofibrils of the fibre. In vertebrates, the neuromuscular junction is an excitatory cholinergic synapse and functions essentially in the same way as any other excitatory cholinergic synapse.

2. (a) The banding pattern results from the overlap pattern of the thick and thin filaments (dark = thick and thin filaments overlapping, light = no overlap).
   (b) **I band**: Becomes narrower as more filaments overlap and the area of non-overlap decreases.
   H zone: Disappears as the overlap becomes maximal (no region of only thick filaments).
   Sarcomere: Shortens progressively as the overlap becomes maximal.

3. Protects the muscle from friction and provides structural integrity to the muscle tissue. The perimysium (surrounding the fascicles) may also be involved in transmitting contractile movements across the muscle.

4. The all-or-none response refers to the way in which an individual muscle fibre contracts maximally (if the stimulus is strong enough) or not at all (if it is not).

5. Without dystrophin there is no structural link between the muscle fibres and the extracellular matrix. Calcium penetrates the plasma membrane (sarcolemma) of the muscle cells and damages them, eventually destroying the muscle cells (fibres).

The Sliding Filament Model (page 325)

1. (a) **Myosin**: Has a moveable head that provides a power stroke when activated.
   (b) **Actin**: Two protein molecules twisted in a double helix shape that form the thin filament of a myofibril.
   (c) **Calcium ions**: Bind to the blocking molecules, causing them to move and expose the myosin binding site.
   (d) **Troponin-tropomyosin**: Bind to actin molecule in a way that prevents myosin head from forming a cross bridge.
   (e) **ATP**: Supplies energy for flexing of the myosin head (power stroke).

2. (a) By changing the frequency of stimulation, so that fibres receive impulses at a greater rate (frequency summation).
   (b) By changing the number and size of motor units recruited (a few motor units = a small contraction, maximum number of motor units = maximum contraction).

3. (a) Calcium ions and ATP.
   (b) Calcium ions are released from a store in the sarcoplasmic reticulum when an action potential arrives. ATP is present in the muscle fibre and is hydrolysed by ATPase enzymes on the myosin.

Types of Muscle (page 326)

1. Smooth muscle, also called involuntary muscle, has spindle shaped cells with one central nucleus per cell and a smooth appearance with no striations. Its contractions are diffuse and it is not under conscious control so it is involved in movement of visceral organs such as the gut.
   Striated (skeletal) muscle is voluntary and is responsible for the skeletal muscle movement over which we have conscious control. It has a striated or striped appearance. The cells are multinucleate with peripheral nuclei.
   Cardiac muscle is involuntary muscle responsible for the contraction of the heart muscle. Although it is striated, it does not fatigue in the same way as skeletal muscle (it has a built in refractory or rest period). There is one nucleus per cell and electrical junctions called intercalated discs join individual cells (rapid transmission of action potentials).

2. Fast twitch fibres are lFarge and pale, they contract rapidly and produce ATP rapidly. They generate a lot of power. They work anaerobically and fatigue quickly. They are suited to short maximal bursts of energy (e.g. sprinting). Slow twitch fibres are darker due to myoglobin, small in diameter and produce ATP more slowly, The rate of contraction is slower. They work aerobically and fatigue slowly so are suited to endurance activity.

Energy for Muscle Contraction (page 327)

1. Lactic acid quickly builds up as a waste product of the glycolytic pathway. Lactic acid inhibits glycogen breakdown and impedes muscular contraction, so the time period for its use is limited.

2. **Energy systems**:
   ATP-CP
   ATP supplied by: Breakdown of CP
   Duration of ATP supply: Short (3-15 s)
   Glycolytic
   ATP supplied by: Anaerobic breakdown of glycogen
   Duration of ATP supply: A few minutes at most.
   Oxidative
   ATP supplied by: Complete aerobic (oxidative) breakdown of glycogen to CO_2 and water.
   Duration of ATP supply: Prolonged but dependent on ability to supply oxygen to the muscles (fitness).

3. (a) Shaded region **A**: Oxygen deficit: the amount of oxygen needed for aerobic supply but not supplied by breathing i.e. an oxygen deficit builds up.
   (b) Shaded region **B**: Oxygen debt: the extra oxygen required (taken in) despite the drop in energy demand. The debt is used to replace oxygen reserves, restore CP, and break down lactic acid.
   Note: Both components (deficit and debt) are often used synonymously (as oxygen debt) although they are not quite the same. The deficit is the oxygen shortfall incurred during exercise; the debt is the amount of oxygen required to restore oxygen and energy stores to resting levels. Their values are not necessarily the same.

4. Oxygen uptake does not immediately return to resting levels because of the extra oxygen required to restore oxygen and energy levels (the oxygen debt).

5. Oxygen supply is increased by increased rate and depth of breathing (increasing gas exchange rate) and increased blood flow (increased gas transport).

6. Lactic acid levels in the blood rise for a time after exercise because the lactic acid is transported in the blood from the muscles (where it has accumulated) to the liver, where it is metabolised to CO_2 and water.

Fight or Flight (page 329)

1. The body's short term response to stress is adaptive because it readies the body for the extra work it might have to do in terms of increased breathing rate, heart rate, and muscular activity. It prepares the body to most efficiently flee or defend itself.

2. Nervous input through the hypothalamus and hormones are both important in coordinating the stress response. Nervous input through sensory stimulation (e.g. getting a fright) stimulates sympathetic nervous system release of catecholamines from the adrenal medulla (hormones such as noradrenaline), bringing about dilation of blood vessels, mobilisation of glucose, and increased heart rate and blood pressure. Continued stress recruits further hormonal response, triggering release of ACTH from the pituitary (mediated again by the hypothalamus) and bringing about the release of glucocorticoids from the adrenal cortex. These mediate suppression of the immune system and metabolism of fats and proteins.

KEY TERMS: Word Find (page 330)

B	O	I	D	Y	T	S	T	N	E	U	R	O	T	R	A	N	S	M	I	T	T	E	R	S
R	N	F	L	C	A	R	D	I	A	C	M	U	S	C	L	E	W	P	G	J	S	S	S	L
A	E	U	K	D	X	F	C	M	M	E	D	U	L	L	A	O	B	L	O	N	G	A	T	A
I	U	N	E	U	R	O	N	E	L	D	G	M	Z	N	W	P	I	N	I	H	Q	U	Z	B
N	R	P	P	N	C	W	R	K	K	C	E	R	E	B	E	L	L	U	M	A	C	T	I	N
S	O	A	U	T	O	N	O	M	I	C	N	E	R	V	O	U	S	S	Y	S	T	E	M	F
Y	M	Z	G	N	O	L	S	Q	A	R	B	R	S	M	O	O	T	H	M	U	S	C	L	E
M	U	R	G	F	D	N	R	Z	A	E	R	E	X	S	Y	N	A	P	S	E	E	N	K	H
P	S	K	E	L	E	T	A	L	M	U	S	C	L	E	L	G	F	D	G	J	D	O	V	I
A	C	A	J	L	Z	P	D	V	R	R	P	I	I	P	E	R	I	P	H	E	R	A	L	W
T	U	A	Y	U	N	H	Y	P	O	T	H	A	L	A	M	U	S	B	A	S	H	T	M	M
H	L	M	P	A	R	A	S	Y	M	P	A	T	H	E	T	I	C	F	O	F	F	B	R	Y
E	A	Y	A	D	A	D	R	N	S	A	R	C	O	M	E	R	E	N	J	P	O	Y	E	O
T	R	F	P	N	V	P	C	E	R	E	B	R	U	M	J	H	Z	F	K	K	U	M	N	S
I	T	S	L	I	D	I	N	G	F	I	L	A	M	E	N	T	T	S	C	C	C	O	I	I
C	R	U	V	O	L	U	N	T	A	R	Y	M	U	S	C	L	E	B	M	K	F	B	Y	N
C	E	N	T	R	A	L	N	E	R	V	O	U	S	M	Y	O	F	I	B	R	I	L	S	T

The Components of Behaviour (page 332)

1. **Innate** behaviour has a genetic basis: It is present from birth and does not need to be learned. **Learned** behaviour results from the experiences of the animal, i.e. existing behaviours are modified as a result of experiences (may be imprinting, conditioning, habituation, imitation, or higher level cognition).

2. (a) A releaser triggers the operation of the innate behavioural program that results in the predictable, stereotyped behavioural response (the FAP).
   (b) Many examples are possible, including those we may have all observed in domestic pets (opening car door = barking, opening refrigerator = meowing). The most striking FAPs are those that occur when animals interact with conspecifics in courtship, territory defense, or dominance encounters. The releaser and the FAP form a signaling system; signaling is the primary purpose of such behaviours. Good illustrative examples include:
   - Red belly models (releaser) in three-spined sticklebacks eliciting the attack response (the FAP) in male sticklebacks.
   - Speckling and (green) color (releaser) eliciting egg rolling behaviour (the FAP) in herring gulls.
   - Bill shape and red patch (releaser) eliciting pecking behaviour (the FAP) in herring gull chicks.

Simple Behaviours (page 333)

1. A **kinesis** describes movement of a cell or organism in which the rate of movement depends upon the intensity (rather than direction) of the stimulus. An example is the increased activity of body lice when temperature increases over 30°C. In contrast, a **taxis** is a directional movement in response to an external stimulus. An example is the negative phototaxis of maggots.

2. Such simple behaviours allow an animal to continue making random orientation responses until it is in an environment that is favorable to its survival (e.g. body lice must reach an appropriate host, as indicated by the surface skin temperature). Once positioned, the behaviour will cease until environmental conditions change once again.

3. (a) Gravi – Gravity
   (b) Hydro – Water/moisture/humidity
   (c) Thigmo – Touch
   (d) Photo – Light
   (e) Chemo – Chemical
   (f) Thermo – Heat

4. (a) A Snails: Negative gravitaxis
   (b) B Moth: Positive chemotaxis
   (c) C Louse: Kinesis in response to temperature
   (d) D Lobster: Positive thigmotaxis
   (e) E Mosquitoes: Positive thermotaxis
   (f) F Maggots: Negative phototaxis

5. 30°C

Primate Behaviour (page 334)

1. Primate sociality has many benefits. The student's discussion could include:

- Group living and a period of prolonged infant dependency increases the amount of time that young primates spend in very close contact with older ones, allowing the transfer of learned behaviour (the development of culture). Group living facilitates inter-generational exchange of information.
- Group living offers greater opportunity for cooperative hunting and group defence, both of which are important to individual and group survival and success.
- Social hierarchies organise groups and allow for a cohesive structure that minimises conflict and improves the efficiency of group behaviours such as foraging.
- Social bonding behaviours, such as grooming, promotes group cohesion and is important in relieving stress, especially for lower ranked individuals.

Learned Behaviour (page 335)

1. (a) The **innate** component of the behaviour is in the **following** response shown to the first object they encounter moving away.
   (b) The **learned** component is that where the young learn to **identify** the type of animal or object to which they are to make a (following) response.

2. Differences between classical and operant conditioning ((a) and (b) any two of in any order)

   - Classical conditioning forms an association between two stimuli (the conditioned and the unconditioned stimulus). Operant conditioning forms an association between a stimulus (reward) and a response.
   - In classical conditioning, the responses are elicited, i.e. subject does not control the sequence of events. In operant conditioning, responses are emitted by the subject, i.e. the sequence of events is contingent on the responses of the subject.
   - In operant conditioning, the experimenter can shape the learning process by reinforcing and enhancing some of the subject's responses but not others. This is not possible with classical conditioning.

3. Operant conditioning is probably the predominant way in which animals learn in their natural environment. Examples could include:

- Sparrows have learned that fluttering in front of the sensors of automatic doors provides them access inside where food is available.
- Young mammals learn to perfect their motor movements through play behaviours.
- Many birds learn to associate dropping shelled food items on to hard surfaces with improved access to the food inside (e.g. thrushes and snails, seagulls and mussels, rooks and walnuts).
- Birds learning to avoid distasteful insects with a particular colouration.

4. Habituation is adaptive because it prevents continued responses to stimuli that provide no reinforcement (reward or punishment). This (1) prevents sensory overload and (2) enables animals to respond to the stimuli that are associated with a consequence.

5. Latent learning is critical to survival where it is associated with behaviours such as navigation and homing, or acquisition of food. Such behaviour enables an animal to correctly locate certain resources based on the total configuration of landmarks in the

environment, e.g. location of food caches in squirrels and nutcracker birds. Cooperative hunting in pack carnivores, such as hunting dogs, probably also includes some elements of latent learning.

Learning to Sing (page 337)

1. (a) In white-crowned sparrows, birds older than 4 months are no longer receptive to further modification of the song.
   (b) Birds deafened as juveniles, even after being exposed to adult song, cannot produce a normal song (only a variable call with no phrasing).
   (c) Birds are capable of producing a simple but phrased song (which is never-the-less recognisably that of a white-crowned sparrow) even when isolated or exposed to the songs of other species during the period of song development. This shows that a certain component of the species song is innate. Young birds exposed to the song of conspecifics during the song development period then learn to modify this basic pattern to sing a fully phrased normal adult song.

2. The ability to modify an innate song pattern by learning has consequences for an individual in terms of attracting a mate over rivals. In evolutionary terms, birds more capable of attracting mates because they can modify and develop a song pattern will pass on this aspect of fitness to their offspring and their genes will have greater representation in later generations.

Insight Behaviour (page 338)

1. Insight learning occurs when there is a mental leap from not knowing to knowing without any physical trials of concepts. It involves the application of reason and logic to develop an answer to a problem. Trial and error requires the physical manipulation of objects to perform a task and the learning develops as a result of the failures and successes that occur.

2. Insight learning is difficult to test because the subject must not have been exposed to a similar problem before testing and the test can not be repeated on the same individual (as this would then involve experience or learning by trial and error). Care must also be taken to make sure other potential subjects do not see the first subject attempting or completing the task.

3. When an animal in the wild is presented with a new problem, such as how to capture a new type of mobile prey item, it may have only one chance to solve it. If the animal can make a reasoned decision as to the best way to complete the task without a trial, it will save energy and gain a competitive advantage.

Dopamine and Behaviour (page 339)

1. Behaviour is based on both genetics and the environment. Although genes may predispose a person to behaving in a certain way, the environment plays a major part in whether or not that behaviour is carried out. In addition, interactions between genes influence their final expression in the phenotype, so it becomes difficult to identify which gene is the 'cause' of the behaviour. Diet also has a major effect on behaviour (through physiological mechanisms) with many studies showing that artificial colourings and flavourings can affect behaviour in young people. Finally, human thought must be included. Humans can consciously alter their behaviour in response to peer pressures and societal expectations (although again, both the environment and genetics play a part in this process).

2. Different dopamine levels are directly associated with certain behaviours. Low levels may cause people to become highly active. Dopamine levels increase when active and give the body a sense of wellbeing and satisfaction. In order to achieve this feeling, people with naturally low levels are often more active than normal as the body tries to produce more dopamine. Low levels are also associated with tendencies towards addiction, as the feelings gained from certain drugs are interpreted by the body as similar to dopamine and there is a physiological craving to maintain the feeling. High levels of dopamine are associated with fixation on certain objects and increased perception of the senses in a way that may cause people to hear and see things in an exaggerated way. Extremely high levels are associated with schizophrenia (a split between what is real and what is not) where the body begins to hear and see things that are not there.

3. Natural variations in the DRD4 gene affect its ability to produce receptors that bind with dopamine. Protein chains that are too long do not fold correctly and produce receptors that do not efficiently bind to dopamine. In this case the body will perceive the levels of dopamine to be low and act in a way to increase them (frequently by increasing activity).

4. Dopamine is present in a number of neural pathways. The link between the DRD4 gene and dopamine levels allows us to theorise that other neural pathways are affected by similar receptor genes. The link between a behaviour and a gene sets a precedence for finding other genes that affect behaviour. It lends weight to the theory that human behaviour is more influenced by genetics than by the environment.

NOTES